THE STORY OF
FAITH

THE STORY OF
FAITH
A move of God... a global result

Garry Rodgers

The Story of Faith
Published by Faith Bible College
with Castle Publishing Ltd
New Zealand

© 2023 Garry Rodgers

ISBN 978-0-473-63857-3 (Softcover)
ISBN 978-0-473-63858-0 (Epub)
ISBN 978-0-473-63859-7 (Kindle)

Editing:
Marie Anticich

Production & Typesetting:
Andrew Killick
Castle Publishing Services
www.castlepublishing.co.nz

Cover Design:
Paul Smith

Scripture quotations marked (KJV)
are taken from the King James Version. Public domain.

Scripture quotations marked (NKJV)
are taken from the New King James Version.
Copyright© 1982 by Thomas Nelson, Inc.
Used by permission. All rights reserved.

Scripture quotations marked (NASB)
are taken from the New American Standard Bible®
Copyright © 2020 by The Lockman Foundation.
Used by permission.

ALL RIGHTS RESERVED

No part of this publication may be reproduced,
stored in a retrieval system, or transmitted
in any form or by any means, electronic, mechanical,
photocopying, recording or otherwise,
without prior written permission from the publisher.

It was prophesied by David du Plessis that we were going to start an end-time training centre and we were going to use the word FAITH in its name. We took hold of that. FAITH comes by hearing and hearing by the Word of God. As Christian believers, we can learn much from the Jewish understanding of FAITH. Because, to Jewish people, FAITH means obeying what you hear. It comes to you from a word (rhema) *– a quickened word that comes from God.*

– Dr Des Short, 2021

Foreword

When I was first asked to write the foreword for this delightful book, I was initially a little hesitant because I had never met the author, Garry Rodgers. But as soon as I started reading the draft of *The Story of Faith*, I was stirred and I began to be intrigued by the kingdom connections and the invisible hand of God that wove the amazing journey of Des and Carley Short and Faith Bible College (FBC). The more I read, the more faith was inspired in me and I knew I had to take on this assignment.

This book faithfully traces the invisible hand of God in the daily affairs of His children, skilfully guiding them step by step along life's arduous journey. The end result is a beautiful tapestry of God's mighty and sovereign hand, weaved delicately into the lives of His chosen vessels.

I first encountered Rev Des Short as a student in Singapore at the Tung Ling Bible School, way back in 1981. Des was teaching on the Song of Songs, and it was the gentleness and sweetness which exuded from him that made us all fall in love with Jesus again. Tung Ling Bible School was established in 1978 and has since seen almost 6,000 students graduate, many of whom have gone on to establish significant churches and ministries all over the world. But what is lesser known is that the school was a direct product of Des and FBC's involvement. The original curriculum of the school was developed with the help of FBC and along with a few brethren from New Zealand and Singapore, a powerful vision was birthed that has now become a massive global blessing.

Another beautiful part of this tapestry is the mention of my spiritual father, the late Dr Brian Bailey. Brother Bailey, an impeccable and godly Englishman who probably made the single greatest impact in my life, was an inaugural lecturer at Faith Bible College and he was a true prophet of God. He often told me stories of what God did in New Zealand during the ten years he was there, and true to form, New Zealand saw a massive move of the Holy Spirit that witnessed many powerful and anointed ministers shot out as arrows into the nations. Singapore has been a definite and direct recipient of that outpouring.

I was deeply impacted as a student at Tung Ling Bible College and those short three months crystallised the call of God in my life. Many years later, beyond my wildest imaginations, God led me and my congregation to purchase, redeem, and fully restore the iconic Bible College of Wales in Swansea, a college that Mr Rees Howells, that great Welsh intercessor, founded in 1927. I have no fear of exaggeration to say that Mr Howells and those praying saints at the Bible College of Wales altered the course of World War II on their knees. What a privilege it is to be part of this amazing narrative.

It is amazing how a single pebble dropped into the pond of God's vast love has had such a vast and profound ripple effect in so many lives. What you have in your hand is a wonderful historical narration of God's goodness through a couple who gave themselves to serve God and who trusted in His unfailing love. This will go into the archives of heaven and when we finally get there, we will all realise how much the invisible, and sometimes visible, grace of God has accompanied us on all our journeys.

To Des and Carley Short, thank you for being faithful servants of the Most High in this incredible journey. We salute you both. And to Garry Rodgers for narrating a true and beautiful record of God's Goodness.

Rev Yang Tuck Yoong
Chairman of the Board, Tung Ling Bible School, Singapore
Director, The Bible College of Wales, Swansea

Des and Carley Short, the founders of Faith Bible College in Tauranga, New Zealand

Contents

Introduction	13
Part 1: A Global Harvest	**15**
Faith	17
Spiritual Spine	25
Another Man	33
A God Idea	39
This is God	47
To Be Like Jesus	57
The Glory	63
That's All I Can Do!	71
This is That	79
Fired Up	87
Faith In Action	95
Fully Impacted	103
The Days of Elijah	113
Atmosphere of Glory	121
Graduates Impacting the World	129
Never Say Never	145
Now It Will Spring Forth	155

Part 2: A Whole New Book – *Positioning for the Coming Harvest* 161
A Mum's Intuition 163
Draw It Near 169
Free Like a Dove 175

About the Author 182

Introduction

I had never even been to Faith Bible College when I was asked to write a book to be called *The Story of Faith*. Over the years I had heard snippets of the stories surrounding Faith, met many graduates and been impacted by the Faith Bible College Correspondence Course. I had often been encouraged in my Christian walk by graduates of Faith and I had even visited a Bible school running the Faith curriculum in Ghana.

But it wasn't until May 2021 that I finally made it over the entrance cattle-stop to Faith Bible College in Tauranga.

Here I found Dr Des Short who was still Principal at the age of 90! But Des, since retired from that position, has been much more than the Principal of a Bible school.

For more than 50 years he operated in the office of Apostle, Prophet and Teacher. In Des and his wife Carley's case, these terms are not just titles of honour. This couple were not five-fold ministry 'wannabes'. They had truly walked in these offices. They had taught and commissioned thousands of students and sent them around the world like arrows in the hand of the Master.

I returned home from Faith Bible College with a wad of old magazines, files and notes. To be quite honest, the task overwhelmed me. I didn't know where to start.

How can one do justice to recount the work of the Holy Spirit through the nearly 5,000 graduates and many staff members of Faith Bible College? You can't. And if you tried to document it all, miracle after miracle, it could actually become quite tedious to read.

So I didn't even attempt to do that. I decided I could only touch on certain aspects that had touched and impacted me in the hope they will also impact you, the reader.

I have endeavoured to tell the story of the prophetic foundation of Faith – Des and Carley's adventure of faith and where it sits in the history of the Church in New Zealand.

I've tried to tell a little of some of the early key staff members; a few inspirational examples of how God has used former graduates; the atmosphere; the Bible schools and missions training centres founded and supported, and the impact of Faith Bible College on the nations.

Des's generation is passing. We, the next generation, are now the harvesters of the seeds his generation has sown. There is no Plan B. Scary? Well, yes. But we have the Holy Spirit and the resources of heaven to help us.

We need to be prepared in these critical and exciting times, and so I have also endeavoured to share some of Des's prophetic insights about the coming harvest.

As I was writing about the history of the college, history was unfolding before my eyes. In 2021 Faith Bible College was going through its greatest change in 50 years, with the appointment of new leadership. What a privilege to record some of that change as it was happening!

Garry Rodgers

Part One

A Global Harvest

Faith

It may surprise you to learn that the well-known Bible teacher Derek Prince was used as an instrument of God to help found Faith Bible College, even if initially he was a reluctant player in God's plan.

Derek was undoubtedly one of the most eminent Bible teachers of the 20th century. From age 14 he studied Greek and Latin at Eton College. At Kings College, Cambridge University, he received a prestigious Fellowship in Ancient and Modern Philosophy; a scholarship funded him to indulge his passion to study those subjects. He also studied Hebrew and Aramaic at Cambridge and later refined his study of Hebrew at the University of Jerusalem.

All these studies would have been like an academic wasteland had God not have gotten hold of Derek's heart. In 1941 Derek had a powerful personal encounter with Jesus, while serving in the British Army.

God further developed this academic into a man of God when he married Danish missionary, Lydia Christensen, and became father to the eight Jewish orphans they adopted. This experience, and Derek's knowledge of the Bible, gave him an understanding of God's plan for Israel that would eclipse the understanding of many of his Bible teacher peers.

The Story of Faith

After doing missionary work in Kenya, Derek and Lydia settled in the United States, where Derek rapidly grew in popularity as a Bible teacher.

In comparison, Des Short could have been tempted to think he was a nobody. Only, there are no nobodies in the Kingdom of God! We are all sons and daughters of God the Father and brothers and sisters of the King of Kings.

With that knowledge, Des plucked up the courage to make a telephone call to this world-renowned Bible teacher. In the providence of God, a relative of Derek's was a classmate of Des's at the Elim Bible Institute in New York State, and had provided Des with Derek's contact details.

Surely Derek would respond to Des's gush of youthful enthusiasm and invitation to speak at a conference in the beautiful Bay of Plenty town of Tauranga, New Zealand, even though it was a tortuously long trip from Derek's adoptive home in the United States.

Surely the same Holy Spirit that prompted Des to make the telephone call would be witnessing to Derek Prince as they spoke? That was Des's expectation.

But Derek responded: 'Now listen here, young man. I told my God that I will never go and preach anywhere outside of my country unless I know who I am going to be with, and I do not know you and I don't want to know you.' And with that Derek hung up.

Well, that was a sure sign that God wasn't in Des's grandiose idea, wasn't it? We would counsel Des to forget the idea and move on. But no. He had the 'rhema' or spoken word of God in his heart and FAITH in that word drove him on. So Des telephoned Derek again and made the same appeal, only to be met with the same rebuttal.

Faith

Perhaps Des should have changed his approach angle like a pilot trying to land an aeroplane in a severe cross-wind. Maybe God would use someone else to spearhead the move of God that Des was expecting to hit New Zealand.

But no. FAITH is the assurance for what he hoped for and FAITH drove him on to make another audacious phone call. This time, Derek responded by telling Des not to call again.

However Derek Prince did call 'nobody' Des from Down Under. With an admission that would have been difficult for an ex-toffee-nose Eton boy, he said, 'Look, God's really done a number on me. I know I need to come across to New Zealand. We are going to see a move of God that's going to have a global result.'

And so Derek Prince came to the 1967 convention that Des had arranged in Tauranga, a convention which was one of the markers for a move of God in New Zealand that became known as the Charismatic Movement.

And the faith Des exhibited in this encounter set a precedent in the Bible training centre, Faith Bible College, which he and his wife Carley founded in 1969.

By 2021 this Bible college had trained nearly 5,000 graduate students for the global end-time harvest. This was achieved both directly and through its international entity, Faith Bible College International, which had spawned numerous Bible training centres in various parts of the world, including:

- Vladivostok, Eastern Russia
- Singapore (Tung Ling Bible School)
- Kuala Lumpur, Malaysia
- Hong Kong
- Hyderabad, Andhra Pradesh, India

- Siliguri, India (West Bengal, in the foothills of the Himalayas)
- Odisha, India
- Pakistan
- Kumasi, Ghana
- Vietnam

And that's only part of the story of extraordinary expansion in the Kingdom of God. The story includes the planting of a church in Singapore by a former Tung Ling Bible School student that has in turn planted over 150 churches, schools, orphanages and Bible colleges in 16 different bases around the world.

This story includes the planting of a church that has grown into one of the largest churches in India with 50,000 members; and the planting of 2,000 house churches in one particular country. It includes development of a network of churches and a church-planting school in spiritually destitute Europe by a couple who were former students; the founding of a very impacting TV media channel by a former student; and the running of a Bible correspondence course that reaches thousands of school children in Thailand, by another former student.

The story of Faith Bible College encompasses the founding of organisations in Thailand and Germany by a former student to rescue young girls and women sold or trafficked into prostitution.

Another former student has educated thousands of school children and community groups throughout New Zealand on substance abuse and making good life choices.

The story of Faith includes the founding of a residential children's home, a women's shelter and home for babies and infants in India by another couple who were former students... The list goes on. It's an end-time harvest which is truly global.

Faith

The Master Potter shaped Des and Carley and the many helpers who came alongside them with perseverance and a tenacity of faith which has brought about this harvest.

Thoughts to Ponder

1. Des had an inkling, a small thought planted by the Holy Spirit, that Derek Prince should come to New Zealand. To Des it was a 'substance', but it could have been brushed off as just a whimsical thought.
   Do you have any examples in your own life where you have acted on a thought or a feeling without a lot of evidence that it would work out, and it has turned out to be a significant God-thing?

2. Do you have a dream, a thought or a feeling right now that you can't shake off and, after reading Des's experience, you feel you should follow through with?

We are going to see a move of God that's going to have a global result.

– Derek Prince, 1967

Spiritual Spine

In the 1950s Des Short was Youth Director at his home church, Oxford Terrace Baptist, in Christchurch, the largest city in the South Island of New Zealand.

Oxford Terrace Baptist had been an evangelical stalwart in Christchurch for several decades. Like so many strong evangelical churches in those days, the leaders' official theological position was such that they did not believe the miracles, as demonstrated by the workings of the Holy Spirit in the book of Acts, were for our time. Miracles had ceased.

One of their most respected pastors, Rev J.J. North, had as a young man led one of the greatest evangelical revival campaigns ever seen in Christchurch, under R.A. Torrey, in 1902.

While serving as pastor of Oxford Terrace Baptist, Rev North became the most vocal critic of the Smith Wigglesworth campaigns held at the Sydenham Gospel Mission in 1922 and 1924, just a few kilometres across town from Oxford Terrace Baptist.

Rev North then became the founding Principal of the New Zealand Baptist Bible College, a position he held for 20 years. He was also editor of the *New Zealand Baptist* magazine for more than three decades, and president of the Baptist Union of churches for two terms.

And so – although they were revivalists, evangelisers, disciplers and missionary senders of great importance to the Kingdom of God – the theological position that miracles had ceased infused the Baptist movement throughout New Zealand and at Oxford Terrace Baptist Church, for many decades to come.

But God seems to revel in 180-degree turnarounds and, during the Charismatic Movement of the 1960s and 1970s many churches in the Baptist Union were among those most deeply impacted by the Holy Spirit.

The Sydenham Gospel Mission embraced the move of the Holy Spirit at that time and, in fact, had already decided to become a fully Pentecostal church a few months before Wigglesworth came and cemented that position. In 1928 they became the Sydenham Assemblies of God (AOG), affiliated with the American Assemblies of God Church. For many years thereafter, the wider Church in Christchurch regarded them as a sort of cultish oddity.

But for hungry young men and women, such as those in Des's youth group, sneak visits to Sydenham AOG were regarded as seeing heaven on earth. In fact they often sped away on their bicycles as soon as they could at the conclusion of the Sunday evening service at Oxford Terrace Baptist just so they could enjoy the closing moments of the Sydenham AOG service.

The pastor of Oxford Terrace Baptist Church, whom Des loved very much, preached a series of sermons in an attempt to dissuade the young people from visiting Sydenham AOG. He preached from 1 Corinthians 14:40, 'Let all things be done decently and in order' (NKJV).

The assumption was that the Pentecostal church was not doing things decently and in order. In fact it was stated that they were 'swinging from the chandeliers', as the saying goes.

Spiritual Spine

But there were no chandeliers! As Des points out, the pastor should have concentrated on the first and most important part of that verse which says, 'Let all things be done...'

Des was among many who received the Baptism in the Holy Spirit at Sydenham AOG. This didn't come easily. Des and his friends attended 'tarrying' meetings where they would wait upon the Lord over a period of weeks or months before they were baptised in the Holy Spirit. During this waiting period they would seek to become clean vessels, and they were encouraged to covet the spiritual gifts.

Des remembers that at one of these meetings one girl was so overwhelmed by the power of the Spirit that she lay incapacitated and rigid on the floor. They had difficulty getting her into the car to take her home before her curfew. Her parents were not impressed!

Des's future wife, Carley Fergusson – unknown to Des at the time – was a member of Sydenham AOG. While serving in the role of Youth Director at Oxford Terrace Baptist, Des was also working for the Young Men's Christian Association (YMCA), an organisation founded by George Williams in 1844 and dedicated to 'improving the spiritual condition of young men'.

Williams credited the inspiration to found the YMCA to his reading of Charles Finney's 1835 revival lectures. But by the 1960s, the word "Christian" seemed to be almost gone from the YMCA, as the organisation concentrated more on social and, in particular, sporting activities: for instance, the YMCA had much to do with the introduction of the sport of basketball.

In contrast, in the mid-1950s, the YMCA was very much an organisation dedicated to sharing Christ with young men through preaching, teaching and, in Christchurch, through the three camps they held each year. It was at one of those camps that

Des gave his life to Jesus. Every Christmas the YMCA led a carol service on the riverbank adjacent to their complex, seeing this as another opportunity to bring Jesus to the city of Christchurch.

The year 1955 was the 100th anniversary of the World Alliance of the YMCA, and a centennial celebration was to be held in Paris. Young representatives from around the globe were chosen to attend and Des and his assistant to the 18- to 20-year-olds, John Hitchens, were selected to represent the YMCA in New Zealand.

And so these two young men embarked upon the adventure of a lifetime with a tour around the world on a huge ship that took them not only to Paris, but also to many YMCA venues in the United Kingdom and Europe.

The centennial celebration in Paris was the highlight of the trip for Des and John, and it was here they learnt of the original vision of George Williams. Although the organisation had gradually watered down the emphasis on the gospel over the years, for the first 50 years all of its members had to be born-again believers.

But it was a film about the 50th Jubilee in 1905 shown at the centenary that most impacted Des, who has often talked about exactly what he saw. The film included photographs and an accompanying narration of a World Alliance of YMCA's International Committee meeting in an upper room of a large venue in London.

They dealt with committee business hastily so they could join the others in the main auditorium to hear their guest speaker, a famous evangelist who was a former president of a branch of the YMCA in the USA.

As they rushed down the stairs and through the large doors of the auditorium where the guest evangelist was preaching, it was recounted there were an estimated 20,000 young men

Spiritual Spine

lying flat on their faces before God. In the film they could be heard speaking in tongues.

This begs the question: who was the famous evangelist in the film and where was the venue? R.A. Torrey happened to be holding meetings in London between February and June 1905. Did he cross the channel to preach in Paris in May 1905? Or did the film show the World Alliance Committee meeting in a room of the Royal Albert Hall, maybe even planning the 50th Jubilee, on a day Torrey was preaching there? The description of an American evangelist who had also been a president of the YMCA best fits D.L. Moody. But Moody died in 1899.

Interestingly, the YMCA had two Jubilees: one being the 1894 Jubilee in London, which celebrated the founding of the YMCA; the other being the Jubilee of the World Alliance of YMCAs celebrated in Paris in 1905.

But it is generally thought that Moody's final visit to England was in 1892 and so even reference to this being the 1894 Jubilee is tenuous. Maybe the film was a recreation of the August 1881 World Conference in London which coincides with a record of Moody being in England in September of the same year.

In the film, the young men at the conference could be heard speaking in tongues. But 1905 was well before the days of movies with synchronised sound, and speaking in tongues had not become a widespread phenomenon until after the April 1906 Azusa Street revival.

We know this because, in 1908, the great British Pentecostal pioneer Rev A.A. Boddy said that the previous year (1907), he only knew of five or six persons in Great Britain who spoke in tongues.

In spite of the inaccuracies, this part of the film had such an authenticity about it that it had a great impact on Des. Maybe

The Story of Faith

the film makers had included other footage of a large gathering of young men speaking in tongues, such as the George Jefferies Pentecostal meetings in the Royal Albert Hall in the 1930s.

While the stitched-together film may be a bit of a mystery, in a miraculous way God used this film to ignite something in Des. He had never heard about speaking in other tongues before this time and there was something about it that really grabbed him.

Upon Des's return to Christchurch, the fire that ignited him in Paris seemed to spread. Many boys in the YMCA started to get saved. At the Wainui camps some were baptised in the Holy Spirit and spoke in other tongues. There were three intakes of boys each summer and sometimes there would be as many as 100 boys in each intake.

In preparation for summer camps, boys would cut the grass using sickles. One particular year as they were cutting the grass, they suddenly experienced God's presence. The boys lifted up their hands and began worshipping the Lord. Several boys started speaking in tongues even though no-one had told them about the Pentecostal experience.

One young man was so lost in God that he was lifted up from his bed as he worshipped. Sometimes boys with no musical training would receive a gift from the Holy Spirit, enabling them to play beautiful music on the piano. At altar calls during those camps most of the boys were born again.

And what these boys received they took home to their families. They began to talk about it and the talk got back to the chairman of the board of the Christchurch YMCA. The chairman, in turn, summoned Des to a meeting in his office. It didn't take Des long to figure out this wasn't going to be a convivial chat over a cup of tea.

The chairman was angry. He said, 'Listen, I am the Dean

of Christchurch Cathedral. I don't believe in salvation!' He scolded Des for having altar calls and told him that young people didn't have to make decisions to go to heaven.

Opening a drawer he took out a cigarette, lit it and blew smoke into Des's face as if to intentionally insult him.

The chairman continued, 'You see you have created a problem, because most of the ones who go to the YMCA are Anglicans as far as church is concerned. You are not to talk about Jesus because it will put the kids off coming to the YMCA.'

Des found this to be a demoralising experience and realised that as he continued his work at the YMCA he had to be very careful. But God was building spiritual spine into Des.

Thoughts to Ponder

1. The Church has changed so significantly in Des and Carley's lifetime, it can be hard to imagine what it was like back then. If the Lord has led the Church so far in their lifetime, think of how the Lord wants to take the Church even further into maturity in your lifetime.

    As the Lord shows you what He wants to do in His Church, share it with others, and together pray into those things.

2. It was just a small thing, a film, that impacted Des in 1955. The film may not have even been a totally accurate representation of history. But it introduced him to the fact that tongues and other gifts of the Holy Spirit didn't cease 2,000 years ago.

    Can you think of some of the small or even peculiar

things that have opened your eyes to the workings of the Holy Spirit?

Another Man

In 1959 the renowned American evangelist, Billy Graham, held a number of meetings around New Zealand. Billy had a deep respect for the work of the YMCA and, on coming to Christchurch, visited the local branch of the YMCA and held a meeting with staff. Des was privileged to be at that meeting.

A crowd of 133,000 (cumulative) turned up at Lancaster Park during the eight-day Christchurch campaign, which began on April 1, 1959. People were hungry to hear the gospel and eager to hear Billy Graham.

This campaign had widespread support from churches of most denominations and was a key element to the unifying work that the Spirit of God was initiating in the Body of Christ. Graham himself preached at the last two meetings.

Although Des had already given his life to Christ, he went forward on an altar call along with a mass of people, to rededicate his life to Christ.

In late 1959 through to mid-1960, another American evangelist, Alvin S. Worley, held meetings in various parts of New Zealand. Worley rented a large theatre in Christchurch near the YMCA and held meetings every night.

He visited the YMCA and said to the General Secretary, 'I like to relax during the day and one of the ways I like to relax is by playing table tennis. Do you have anyone who can play table tennis with me?'

Des Short could play table tennis quite well and was 'volunteered' for the job. So, daily, A.S. Worley would show up at lunchtime and challenge Des to a game of table tennis. Although Des played consistently, he lost every time. But Worley took a keen interest in Des and the time they spent together was God ordained.

When you spoke to A.S. Worley one-to-one he was not impressive at all. But when he spoke in a meeting, suddenly the Spirit of God would come upon him in a powerful way and the glory of God would manifest in his meetings. 'It was almost as if he became another man,' Des remarked. 'Amazing signs and wonders took place.'

Worley invited Des to come to his meetings. Des didn't really want to go but felt he should as Worley had been kind to him. When Des entered the theatre, Worley was on the platform. Before he preached, he shared some of his life story: how he came from a very poor family and, as a 13-year-old, had to leave school before attending high school so he could work to feed his family.

'Goodness gracious me!' Des thought. Worley's story really cut into his heart and, even today, he says, 'Worley's story was so dear. It was dear.' While relating the story of his life, Worley suddenly stopped and asked Carley Fergusson, who was on the platform, to sing.

Introducing her, he said she sang every night on the international shortwave station HCJB, broadcasting from Quito Ecuador. From that day on, Des became so star-struck or perhaps smitten that he would tune in to listen to Carley sing on HCJB every night.

Carley and her three sisters were part of a group called The Fergusson Sisters, who performed as a trio or sometimes as a quartet. With their brother John in the mix they were known as The Fergusson Five. At one stage, they were very popular, so much so that in 2007 they were retrospectively honoured by being inducted into the Old Time Country Music Hall of Fame.

A relationship developed between Des and Carley, leading to their engagement. Their wedding ceremony was to be held at the Oxford Terrace Baptist Church. They wanted Carley's pastor from the Sydenham AOG church to be involved in the ceremony, but the Baptist pastor didn't want anything to do with the Pentecostal church.

But, through the love of Jesus, Des was able to express what it would mean to him if the Oxford Terrace pastor 'would be so gracious enough', as Des expressed to him, to allow Carley's pastor to come so that the two of them could conduct the wedding ceremony together.

Des's pastor eventually agreed to this and the two of them conducted the ceremony. Des feels this breaking down of a wall of disunity between these two parts of the Body of Christ was very significant. It had never happened before.

Des sees this as quite a prophetic moment in the way God would use both him and Carley in the early days of the Charismatic Movement in New Zealand, where the Holy Spirit would unite both the Pentecostal and the historical denominational churches in a way that man could not do.

Even in those early days, Des and Carley had a Kingdom of God mindset rather than a church mindset. This was essential for what God would call them to do. As a couple they were determined to glorify God, and Carley had Psalm 34:3 inscribed on her wedding ring:

O magnify the Lord with me, and let us exalt his name together. (KJV)

At one of his meetings, A.S. Worley said, 'I know some of you have got problems with your teeth. How many of you have a problem with your teeth?' It was amazing how many put up their hands. He prayed for them and the holes in their teeth were filled with material such as gold or silver.

A sensationalist news tabloid, *The Truth*, reported on this and labelled A.S. Worley a 'charlatan' who should be sent out of the country. To prove their point, *The Truth* brought in a group of top dentists to examine the teeth.

However, the dentists found that the fillings were genuine. Not only did they find they were genuine, but the fillings were absolutely perfect. They remarked that with any filling there was an element of roughness that only a dentist could detect. But these fillings were perfectly smooth with no roughness.

The plan to discredit Worley backfired and he went on to hold meetings in other centres. Some of these meetings could only be described as revival, particularly in the small city of Timaru, where more than 600 people were saved.

Des and Carley wanted to serve as missionaries and had set their hearts on going to South America. However in those days it was difficult for a Pentecostal woman such as Carley to attend one of the main evangelical Bible training colleges in New Zealand. They wouldn't accept her.

Apart from the anti-Pentecostal sentiment of the Baptist Church at the time, the other main evangelical Bible college, the New Zealand Bible Training Institute, had an anti-Pentecostal sentiment following the trajectory set by its co-founder, Joseph Kemp.

Although he was a revivalist and sympathetic to the workings of the Holy Spirit as demonstrated in the Keswick movement, Kemp was another outspoken critic of the Smith Wigglesworth campaign, following the lead of his associate, Rev J.J. North.

In response to their dilemma, A.S. Worley encouraged Des and Carley to take a three-year Bible training course at the Elim Bible Institute at Lima in New York State, USA.

Just ten days after their wedding they departed New Zealand burning their bridges behind them, thinking this would be the launching of their missionary service to South America. But God had a better idea, a God idea!

Thoughts to Ponder

1. A.S. Worley was very much a key person the Lord brought into Des's life at just the right time. Can you think of key people the Lord has brought into your path at just the right time? How does that make you feel about your destiny?

2. If you are a student of revival, do some reading on the cross-pollination between the Welsh Revival and the Azusa Street Revival. Discuss how the Welsh Revival was a spark for many revivals including Azusa Street.
   Investigate how the Azusa Street Revival was the spark for the Pentecostal revival in Wales. Can you think of more recent revivals where you can see such cross-pollination?

Des and Carley's wedding at Oxford Terrace Baptist Church, Christchurch, in 1960. YMCA boys in their 'Y' gym uniforms form a guard of honour.

A God Idea

Des and Carley sailed from New Zealand to New York by ship, and started their course at Elim Bible Training Centre in 1961. Although the intake of students was between 100 and 120 in number, by the end of their course in 1963, only 38 remained.

Most of the students were single and class seating and accommodation were partitioned between the sexes. Other students were envious of Des and Carley's marital status.

When the principal of Elim Bible Institute visited Faith Bible College many years later he was quite shocked that the accommodation blocks had both male and female rooms in the same complex.

However, Des explained that by treating the students as responsible adults, they had risen to the level of trust placed in them. And over the years, they had very few problems with these living and working arrangements.

While studying, Des and Carley were dreaming of their future mission work in South America. In 1962 during their summer break, they were given a taste of what they thought their future might look like. They travelled to British Guiana and Trinidad.

En route the aircraft was diverted, landing in Cuba to pick up refugees just as the Cuban missile crisis was unfolding and many were trying to flee the island.

As the aircraft landed and its door was opened, they were quickly surrounded by men, women and children who were desperate to leave. Des and Carley and other passengers helped as many refugees as they could board the aircraft, and Carley helped mothers and children find seats.

Not long after the aircraft took off, the pilot was ordered to fly back to the terminal and, if they didn't comply, the missiles aimed at them would blow them out of the sky. Des and Carley could see the panic in people's faces.

Just as the aircraft left the ground, Castro's soldiers had reached the airport. When the plane re-landed, soldiers boarded the aircraft, pointed guns at the passengers and ordered them to get off. The Cuban passengers knew they were in trouble and many were panicking and screaming in fear. The refugees were separated from the foreigners, who were escorted to a room where they were held for many hours.

Needless to say there was a lot of prayer from Des, Carley and the other students. Eventually, under the watchful eye of the Cuban army, they were allowed to re-board the aircraft to proceed to British Guiana, but without the refugees.

When they arrived in British Guiana, it was also suffering from political unrest. At this stage it was still a British colony, but communism was making inroads and it looked as if the communists would win control.

Des and Carley saw large groups of citizens roaming the streets, wielding brooms and yelling, 'Sweep them out!' It was becoming dangerous for supporters of the old party and dangerous for foreigners, who they wanted to sweep out of the way.

When protestors gathered around the house where Des and Carley were staying, they retreated to the bedrooms to pray.

Carley remarked on the prayer movement that came against

A God Idea

the rebellion: 'Prayer became an all-prevailing activity among the Christians in the city and we joined them in the Georgetown Cathedral, an old wooden structure in the centre of the city. It hummed with prayer and this was like a cathedral bell ringing out from the people. Thousands of Christians would gather: workers, school children, mothers and the elderly. They cried out to God to save their land.'

The intensity of prayer really struck Carley and, as she later commented, 'I have never been in such an atmosphere with hundreds of people praying, tears streaming down their faces, wrestling with the consequences if God did not intervene. It was an incredible experience.'

It must have seemed as if their prayers hadn't broken through when the Communist government was elected into power. However even at that stage, Carley thought the Communist Party was like a wounded animal and, two years later, they were overthrown. The land never came under Communist rule again.

This was a great lesson on the power of prayer for Des and Carley and was part of the equipping that God was doing in their lives. Although they were keeping their eyes open for opportunities for further mission work, an opportunity just didn't seem to arise. It was a totally different environment to recent times where it has become easier to join a missionary endeavour.

But, in the last days of their time at Elim Bible Institute, very clear direction came.

'We cried out to the Lord,' Des recounts, 'and asked Him to speak to us because we desired with all our hearts to move straight out onto a mission field.'

A few weeks before graduation, to mark the end of their course, students participated in a week of prayer. This culminated in a chapel service.

Two former students who had started a Bible school in British Guiana were invited to speak at the service. They had witnessed a revival break out in their Bible school. The 180 students were quite excited at this meeting because they got to sit in a circle and guys were mixed with girls.

At the end of the meeting, Paul Stutzman, a visiting missionary to the Philippines, was asked to give the benedictory prayer while the group stood in a circle holding hands. As Stutzman prayed, Des couldn't understand why, but he began weeping like a baby. He could see big teardrops splashing onto the parquet wooden floor.

Maybe it was partly because he felt they hadn't received the direction from the Lord they had so earnestly sought. But the Holy Spirit was doing something in the depths of his being.

All of a sudden Des heard footsteps pacing toward him and felt a hand come down on his head. Stutzman laid his hands on him and Carley and began to prophesy. Even though he didn't know Des and Carley were married, this is what he prophesied:

> My son and daughter, I am going to send you back to your own country. I am going to use you to raise up an end-time missions training centre from which literally hundreds upon hundreds of people will be thrust to the four corners of the earth to preach and to demonstrate the reality of the Kingdom of God. And, my son and daughter, I am going to give you a teaching ministry.

At that time one of Des's sayings was 'I can't speak and I can't preach for sour apples.' This colloquial New Zealand saying means that no-one would even pay Des in sour apples for his speaking or preaching.

A God Idea

While he was at Elim Bible Institute he had never been to an outstation to practise speaking and preaching. He had never even been asked to give a testimony.

Carley was often asked by the college staff to go to other meetings and sing. Des would accompany her. One day, he was asked to give a greeting and, after the meeting, a lady at the door shook him by the shoulders and said, 'I really love the sound of your voice.'

Des thought she was half crazy but then thought, 'Ah well, at least they like the sound of my voice!'

Even apart from the very 'out-there' word of raising up an end-time training centre, just the thought of teaching was 'out there' for Des. He was left thinking: 'How can that be?'

Paul Stutzman further explained that the thrusting out of people would be like arrows leaving the bow and hitting the mark. The other students were envious of the word spoken over Des and Carley and flocked around them. They seemed to have more witness to the word than Des and Carley themselves!

But often – even though a word from God may seem to have come out of left field – when we look back, we see how He has been preparing our hearts.

Des and Carley had heard reports of a short-term intensive Bible training programme in Africa. After training, each student would be sent out and would be expected to return with a new convert, who in turn would go through the same training course, before they too were sent out to make new disciples.

As Carley recalled, 'Our hearts were stirred by these reports and we did wonder about the possibility of starting such a work in New Zealand.' But at that stage they did not want to go back to New Zealand as they felt they had burned their bridges behind them.

'This word left us broken before the Lord,' Des recalls. 'We had made up our minds to be missionaries and we had not planned to return and work in New Zealand. But this was a word I had to give obedience to.'

Two weeks later the final graduation service was held. The guest speaker was South African Pentecostal minister, David du Plessis, one of the main founders of the Charismatic Movement.

In 1936, during a preaching tour in South Africa, Smith Wigglesworth had prophesied over du Plessis that God would outpour His Spirit upon the historic churches and that he would be greatly used by God in this.

David du Plessis became like a bridge between the Pentecostal church and the mainline historical churches, particularly the Roman Catholic Church.

At the graduation du Plessis shared an experience of his that Des never forgot. Du Plessis had visited a church in New York State where he'd heard there were problems and some members were trying to get rid of their pastor. When he got there, the elders were talking against their pastor.

When du Plessis informed them he was going to visit the pastor, they said, 'You are not going to go and see him. We are not going to allow you to go!'

The group of men and women were standing around him and some of the men were physically large and intimidating. Deciding to make a run for it, du Plessis raced out of the building and down a path, with the group chasing after him. As he was about to go through the gate, he was lifted up in the Holy Spirit and suddenly found himself knocking on the front door of a house six miles away.

The wife of the very pastor he wanted to pray for opened the door. Inside he could see the pastor lying on a couch, about to take his last breath. Du Plessis prayed for the pastor and he was instantly healed. About an hour later, the group chasing du Plessis caught up to him at the house.

When they learnt what had happened, they repented of their hatred and were reconciled to their pastor. And so, in a very supernatural way, God used du Plessis to bring unity and healing to this church, and similarly used him to establish unity in the Body of Christ internationally.

After du Plessis had spoken to the students he said, 'Now listen. All this time I have been speaking to you, I haven't been able to get my eyes off this couple.' He then walked straight up to Des and Carley and began to prophesy:

> ...I am going to send you back to your own country. I am going to use you to raise up an end-time missions training centre from which literally hundreds upon hundreds of people will be thrust to the four corners of the earth to preach and to demonstrate the reality of the Kingdom of God.

It was almost the exact same prophecy delivered by Paul Stutzman. The Lord was imprinting that word firmly onto Des and Carley's hearts and activating it in the realm of the Spirit.

Furthermore, du Plessis prophesied they would use the word 'FAITH' in the name of the training centre and that New Zealand would become a sending nation.

The next day the Elim Bible Institute Principal, Carlton Spencer, called Des and Carley to his office. Spencer, lecturer Bob Mumford and other members of the faculty told Des and Carley they believed the prophetic word they had been given was from the Lord.

They prayed for them and commissioned them to this work of the Lord. And so, after graduating in August 1963, Des and Carley returned to New Zealand.

Thoughts to Ponder

1. Maybe you have had the experience of thinking you were going to serve the Lord in a particular way and then, through a word or circumstance, He has given you His idea and changed your direction completely. Share your experience with others.

2. What were the characteristics of the prayer of the British Guiana believers, observed by Carley, that enabled them to break through and impact their nation?

3. Smith Wigglesworth spoke a word of apostolic commissioning over David du Plessis, who spoke a word of apostolic commissioning over Des and Carley.
    What is the place of apostolic commissioning in the Body of Christ today?

4. Discuss the power to bring a thing to pass inherent in a prophetic word. What are the limitations to the word being fulfilled?

This is God

Upon their return to New Zealand, Des and Carley accepted an invitation to become pastors of the Otumoetai Assemblies of God Church in Tauranga, later renamed 'The Revival Centre'.

During this time many were born again and there were regular water baptisms in the church. On one occasion 40 people were baptised.

Des and Carley were always encouraging their congregation to go further in God. In fact they encouraged them to become *desperate* for God. One day Des found the letters 'perate' added to the name label on the door of his office. It read: 'Des*perate* Short'. Perhaps Des's emphasis irritated them a bit.

One of Des's sayings is, 'Jesus was not a man-pleaser. He was not a woman-pleaser. He was a Father-pleaser'. God was going to use Des and Carley to cause others to hunger and thirst for more of Him.

In those days, there were no trans-denominational Christian conventions or conferences held in New Zealand. However Des and Carley felt the Lord wanted them to organise a convention in Tauranga.

The first convention was held in 1966, and Des invited Gerald Derstein, one of his fellow students in the USA, to be the main speaker. Before attending Elim Bible Institute, Gerald

The Story of Faith

had been a Mennonite preacher. In their traditional setting, the Mennonites look very similar to the more popularised Amish believers. However the Mennonites do not believe in separation from the world like the Amish.

Gerald Derstein had a gift in leading worship and was talented in playing both organ and piano. Worship was established as a foundation at the very first convention and became an important feature of the conventions that continued for 15 years.

David and Dale Garratt, who founded Scripture in Song in 1968, began assisting with the worship at the Tauranga conferences from 1967. In fact David and Dale's leadership in worship was a very significant catalyst for the Charismatic Movement in New Zealand and internationally.

David Garratt describes how God used them during this period:

> When we began Scripture in Song in the late '60s we heard two words we took as being from the Holy Spirit. One was: 'Sing songs to Me rather than about Me, or about yourselves.'
>
> The other word, which was foundational to our actual leading as we travelled and taught about worship, and taught and led songs, was: 'Lead the people to Me'. From this impression, I never saw the stage as anything like a destination.
>
> But we were to be, as it were, a conduit to point people to the Father. What this meant was that in my leading, without an instrument, I was always listening.
>
> In listening I would change direction any time it seemed that a new direction was being prompted by the Spirit. This could involve a few words of encouragement.

This is God

Or it could involve the singing of a song again, because it seemed as if the Spirit wanted something emphasised by repetition.

On occasions I would turn to a musician and ask them what God was saying to them. This meant that those on stage had to consider themselves and the listeners as well as Dale and myself, because they knew I didn't see them as mere musicians, but as those following the direction of the Spirit with us.

The other thing we were doing was teaching songs, and we did this line by line. I mean we would sing a line and then have the people sing the line.

I found it didn't really take a lot of time. But by the time the people had learned the song it was their own. Then we weren't just singing a song to the people, but with them. I always watched the people in the back rows because if they weren't learning the song as quickly as the people in the front, I would wonder if the song was good enough.

The songs had to be simple, repetitive and memorable because I wanted to be sure that when they left the room, the songs were still with them, so that the Spirit of God could bring them back to their attention and speak to them through the song.

Many people travelled from Auckland, New Zealand's most populous metropolitan area, to that first convention, and in subsequent years there wasn't a hall big enough in Tauranga to host all the attendees. So they hired the Tauranga Racecourse and the grandstands were filled with people hungry for more of God.

In 1967 Derek Prince came to the convention as the main speaker. In fact Derek later commented that this event was the launch of his international ministry. At first Des found it hard to get on with Derek. He was saying some things that Des didn't like. Carley, however, developed a rapport with Derek and kept the communication channels open.

About three days into the ten-day convention, just after the morning meeting, Derek came to Des and said, 'I believe there is a shop called Woolworths in downtown Tauranga. It's a department store. Can you take me there? I want you and Carley to wait in the car and not come out, but to wait for me.'

So Des and Carley took Derek to Woolworths and they waited in the car. Derek went into the store and came out with a paper bag. Des was dying to know what was in it. That night, while David and Dale Garratt were leading the worship, Derek opened up the paper bag and took out a skipping rope. He began skipping. It was a prophetic act of worship.

It was probably going through Derek's mind that if he had shared what he was intending to do, Des and Carley may not have understood: they may have thought Derek had completely lost his marbles. But God was breaking down traditions, and perhaps He was also breaking down Derek Prince's starchiness.

Just as they had finished the worship and got down from the platform, Derek called Carley up and said, 'I want you to sing a song that is coming from the heart.' Carley sang the chorus from the hymn 'He Giveth More Grace' by Annie Flint:

His love has no limit, His grace has no measure,
His power no boundary known unto men,
For out of His infinite riches in Jesus,
He giveth and giveth and giveth again.

Derek then preached from Proverbs 16:24:

> Pleasant words are a honeycomb,
> Sweet to the soul, and healing to the bones. (NASB)

When he finished preaching, he said, 'I am going to have an altar call on this tomorrow morning and I want any of you who are here, particularly those who have problems with their bones, to come for prayer.'

He then came back to Des, glared at him and said, 'I'm finished.'

It was as if he was saying to Des, 'Over to you.' While talking during the lunch break one day, Derek had heard a little about the prophetic words spoken over Des and Carley and sensed it was time to share the vision.

So Des went up to the microphone and shared the vision of planting an end-times missions training centre and the two prophetic words that had been spoken over him and Carley by Paul Stutzman and David du Plessis.

All of a sudden, just as he was speaking, Des felt what he thought was the Lord's hand on him. Maybe it was, but it wasn't just the Lord; it was also Derek Prince moving him away from the microphone.

As he kept one hand on Des, Derek said, 'I want to say something to you. Everywhere I go, the church leaders or the people who have invited me are always asking for money from the people. They use me to make money. I find it so hard. But I come to Kiwiland, New Zealand, and this man and his wife have never asked us for anything. Just once a day they'll take up a love offering for the meeting. I've never experienced that before.'

And Derek was almost weeping as he said, 'But I love it. I

love it.' He continued, 'Most of you are in beach clothing. But what I would like you to do – and I've never done this before – is to just put your hands in your pockets and take out whatever offering you have. There's a table here in front. I just want you to put money on the table to indicate to this couple that you are standing with them.'

People came forward and gave their money and when it was counted, it added up to exactly £7,000, not a penny less and not a penny more.

Derek went up to the pulpit the next morning and said, 'This is God. I told this young man I was not going to come. I am so glad that God got me here.' He announced the figure that had been raised. Immediately someone in the audience jumped up and said, 'I'll double it.'

And so, Faith Bible College started with £14,000, which is equivalent to about $540,000 today but in terms of property inflation, worth much more.

But that wasn't the end of the skipping saga. One morning, Des and Carley were awoken to a *thud... thud... thud* in the kitchen and when they checked it out, there was Derek Prince, skipping again.

In 1968 Des started looking for a property to start this college called FAITH. All he had for transport was a bicycle. One day he decided to bike 16 kilometres from Otūmoetai in Tauranga to Welcome Bay. He decided to go there just because he liked the sound of the name: 'Welcome Bay'.

Des ended up by the fence of a beautiful 60-acre farm. He jumped over the fence, took a ten-cent coin out of his pocket, held it up before the Lord and said, 'Lord, will you go with me while I approach the people who own this property?'

Des then went up to the beautiful brand-new farmhouse and

knocked on the door. He said to the man who opened the door, 'Are you considering in any way selling this property?'

The man was drunk. He cursed Des and said, 'You get the hell off this property. My wife and I have been buying and selling property for years and each time we sell, we get more than what we are actually wanting, because we get more than the figure we are quoting. And my wife is finally in a house that she loves. I am not going to quote any figure to you.'

Des took a business card out of his pocket and said, 'Look. I'll give you this just in case circumstances change, because sometimes circumstances change that cause people to leave their property and if you are ever going to sell it, we would be very happy to buy it.'

The landowner replied, 'This is my wife's dream house and we are not going to sell it to anybody!'

A few weeks later Des got a telephone call. Something had happened in the man's family and because of this family situation, they were having to pack up and leave Tauranga.

Currency had changed from pounds to dollars in New Zealand in 1967, and so the landowner gave Des a dollar figure to purchase the property: $50,000. And so they bought the property. Four ten-acre lots were sold to fund building on the remaining land.

Thoughts to Ponder

1. David and Dale's worship leading revolutionised church worship and became a foundation for the way worship was led in churches for decades to come.

How well do you think we do these days in fulfilling the desire of the Holy Spirit when He spoke: 'Sing songs to Me rather than about Me or about yourselves' and 'Lead the people to Me'?

Worship songs are now often very complex. Is there a place for worship songs that are 'simple, repetitive and memorable' today?

2. Notice how Des didn't just wait for the word to be fulfilled, he went looking. Do you have a promise from the Lord, where, to be honest with yourself, you haven't been seriously looking for His answer?

3. Notice how when Des stepped out (or in his case, biked out) it seemed that he was being rebuffed. But then looking back, it was as if the Lord had already prepared the way and was in fact ordering his steps.

Does this make you think that perhaps a rebuff, a negative reaction or a door that seems to close before you are often not good indicators of whether or not God is working on the answers in your situation? Pray for eyes to see God ordering your steps.

Faith Bible College campus pictured in the early 1970s

To Be Like Jesus

The initial vision was that God was going to use Faith Bible College to raise up end-time leaders who would manifest courage for the Lord Jesus and who would minister in the supernatural power of the Holy Spirit.

When the ministry of Faith Bible College commenced, Des began to interact with various church leaders, and he came to see what some leaders in churches were really like. Many weren't there to serve, but to be served.

He didn't want students who went through Faith to end up like that. He wanted them to be like Jesus, who was a servant leader. So the mission statement was modified so that the emphasis was on producing servant leaders. The mission statement became:

To prepare servant leaders for the end-time global harvest, who manifest the character of Christ and who minister in the supernatural power of the Holy Spirit.

The annual conventions continued for 15 years with various keynote speakers. One of their favourite speakers was the aforementioned Bob Mumford, who was based as a teacher at Elim Bible Institute in the USA, where Des and Carley had trained between 1961 and 1963.

The Story of Faith

Mumford had a way of saying things that really stirred up his audience in Tauranga. One of his sayings was, 'Lord bless us four, no more, Acts 2:4'.

When he first heard this, Des thought, 'How stupid!' But Des then understood what Bob was on about: believers can take the experience of being filled with the Holy Spirit and waste it on their own little world, without taking it to the needy world beyond them, as the Lord intends.

As well as Des and Carley, many others poured out their lives to make the conventions happen and to get Faith Bible College up and running. The Lord also began to draw various teaching staff to assist.

In 1968 Des contacted the principal of Elim Bible Institute and asked if they would be able to supply the right person to come to assist in leading the new college in Tauranga.

Dr Brian Bailey, a man gifted in the prophetic ministry, felt the Lord direct him to come and assist Des with lecturing at Faith Bible College in its first year of operation, in 1969.

Dr Bailey shared what the Lord had told him at that time: 'The Lord spoke to me in a vision concerning Faith and, in fact, the whole nation of New Zealand. He showed me arrows leaving New Zealand and going to many parts of the world. With this vision came the admonition, "Make of My sons and daughters in New Zealand – ARROWS in My hand!"'

While Dr Bailey was based at Faith, God gave him dreams nearly every night, mostly concerning college students. He knew he had a responsibility to share what he was seeing with the students, but he would only meet to share if a local leader was present.

Des was often called upon to sit in on those sessions and he would quietly pray in the Spirit while Dr Bailey counselled and ministered.

Dr Bailey soon developed a reputation in Tauranga and others outside the college also sought his counsel. The Lord would often give him a word for the person. Sometimes, if he didn't get a word from the Lord, he would lay his hands on the person and he always knew that when he laid his hands on them, the Lord would open his eyes.

The students feared Dr Bailey somewhat. On one particular occasion a church elder and his wife came for a counselling session. The elder was complaining that his wife was an impediment to his ministry.

Dr Bailey spoke what the Lord had shown him: 'Your wife is not the problem. You are! Because, last night at 9.00 pm, you were having sex with another woman.'

The man repented and the Lord did a miracle of healing in their marriage. The revelation of the Holy Spirit is always with the aim of reformation and restoration, which is foremost in the heart of the Father.

When Dr Bailey returned to the USA, he founded Zion Christian University (ZCU). Faith Bible College graduates who wished to further their studies were encouraged to do so through ZCU. There was an agreed credit pathway for Faith Bible College graduates transitioning to the ZCU programme.

In the first year of Faith's operation, 16 students enrolled in the first of three, three-month courses held that year. The former farmhouse was used as a kitchen, dining hall, lecture room and sleeping quarters, supplemented with caravans, while the first accommodation block was built.

Over the next 20 years there was an almost continual building programme at Faith, with the addition of accommodation blocks, houses, apartments, lecture rooms, kitchen, dining hall, a chapel and a prayer house.

Des's early mentor and friend, A.S. Worley, accepted an invitation to teach at Faith in 1969, and stayed the whole year in 1970.

Now, Des was well aware of the way in which the Lord used A.S. Worley to fill people's teeth. He also knew that a staff member, Les Taylor, had problems with his teeth, and he pleaded with Les to come to A.S. Worley's first meeting. Taylor was a bit sceptical but came reluctantly.

A.S. Worley said, 'I wasn't going to pray for anyone to have their teeth filled, but God showed me that he is already filling teeth. If you want God to fill your teeth, come forward so I can lay my hands on you.' Les was at the back, questioning the whole thing in his mind.

But Des embarrassed him by telling him to go forward and, because he was part of Des's staff, he felt he couldn't refuse and went forward. That night, before going to bed, Les was preparing to brush his teeth and got a complete surprise to see pure gold fillings!

There were other miracles which the Lord did in their midst. During a visit to India, Des Short called forward a 14-year-old teenager, Peter Perumalla, who was operating the church sound desk. Des delivered a prophetic word over him.

Peter didn't understand all of that prophetic word at the time but felt God wanted him to go to Faith Bible College in New Zealand. Even before he travelled, Peter suffered from deep vein thrombosis (DVT). For four years he was in a lot of pain, could hardly walk or stand and had difficulty sleeping.

Doctors told him he shouldn't travel by aeroplane as pressurisation could cause a blood clot to develop and travel to his heart and kill him. However, Peter knew God wanted him to go to Faith Bible College and so, against the advice of doctors, he flew to New Zealand in 2002.

Doctors in Tauranga told Peter there was nothing they could do about the DVT that had developed, and that they would have to amputate his leg. Peter's classmates came together in the Prayer House and laid hands on him. That day God healed him completely. Peter Perumalla eventually became a pastor of a church in Auckland, New Zealand, and a guest lecturer at Faith Bible College.

Thoughts to Ponder

1. The distinction between a leader and a servant leader was considered so important it became part of the mission statement. Why is leading as a servant so much more effective?

    As the Holy Spirit leads, examine your own leadership and if necessary, ask Him to help you reset your focus to servant leadership.

2. Dr Brian Bailey's prophetic word, 'Make My sons and daughters in New Zealand – ARROWS in My hand!' was embraced as one of the mottos of Faith Bible College.

    What are the characteristics of arrows that make them a good picture of His servants?

*James Muir (second from left) and Des Short (far right)
engaging with local Māori kaumātua (elders)*

The Glory

Many church movements were birthed through the influence of the 1906 Azusa Street Revival, which had renewed emphasis on the current-day workings of the Holy Spirit, as exhibited in the book of Acts.

The resultant church movements that developed were labelled 'Pentecostal'. For the first 60 years the Pentecostal Movement developed without significantly impacting historic mainline church movements.

But during the 1960s, this began to change as historic churches also began to experience an awakening to the workings of the Holy Spirit. This later awakening within the whole Church is often labelled the 'Charismatic Movement'.

Although of significance, the Tauranga conventions and Faith Bible College weren't the only ways God brought the Charismatic Movement to New Zealand. One of the earliest moves that set the stage for the Charismatic Movement was among the Open Brethren.

In the early 1960s, there was much debate on the Baptism in the Holy Spirit in Open Brethren churches. This was, in part, due to a reaction to the ministry of the Scotsman, Campbell McAlpine, who came to New Zealand in 1959. Hunger for more of the Holy Spirit was fuelled by news of various moves of God in other places.

For instance, Ivor Davies, a missionary with Worldwide Evangelisation for Christ (WEC), inspired hungry believers with reports of the outpouring of the Holy Spirit he had witnessed in the Congo.

At the height of the debate, a well-respected Brethren Bible teacher, Milton Smith, wrote a booklet in support of the Baptism in the Holy Spirit, entitled *Tongues Shall Cease*, causing him to be ostracised by the leaders of the Open Brethren movement.

In 1963 Milton was due to speak at the Brethren-supported Willow Park Christian Camp at Eastern Beach in Auckland. However, because of Milton's stance on the current-day work of the Holy Spirit, the camp committee cancelled his engagement and instead invited another well-respected British Open Brethren teacher and revivalist, Arthur Wallis, to speak.

Unbeknown to them, Arthur had also been baptised in the Holy Spirit. He became another significant catalyst for the Charismatic Movement and spoke at many cottage meetings around the country. In 1964, Arthur organised a meeting at Massey University in Palmerston North with speakers including himself, Milton Smith, Campbell McAlpine and Baptist, Tom Marshall.

This conference was attended by many who were hungry for more of the Holy Spirit and – just like the Tauranga conventions – it was a marker for the Charismatic Movement in New Zealand.

This movement was further cemented after the tour of an American Episcopalian, Father Dennis Bennett, in 1966. His tour had widespread impact on Anglican and other historical churches.

And so the Tauranga convention of 1967, where Derek Prince

The Glory

was the main speaker, was right on the threshold of that movement. Spirit-filled believers were hungry to hear teaching from the Word of God that flowed from Derek. It was God's perfect timing.

Upon the resignation of a lecturer at Faith Bible College, Milton Smith was asked to step in temporarily to fill the gap. For 15 months, every Friday afternoon, Milton would travel from his home in Auckland to Tauranga to give lectures on Saturdays.

Although Milton very much loved his work as Mathematics Head of Department at Auckland Grammar School, one of New Zealand's most prestigious secondary schools, he felt God calling him to teach at Faith Bible College.

He resigned his teaching position and commenced teaching full-time at Faith Bible College in 1974, until his retirement in 1983.

Students said that watching Milton with his wavy white hair look up to heaven while delivering his lectures without notes, was like watching Moses.

Over a period of 20 years, Milton wrote a study series on the Bible called *Knowing God in His Word*. That study series was run as a correspondence course from Faith Bible College, with the support of Milton's family. It grounded many Christians, who weren't able to attend a Bible college, in the Word of God.

Milton maintained some of the Open Brethren perspectives on the Word of God. He would light up when talking about plurality in leadership – shared responsibility and accountability by a number of leaders – in the Body of Christ. In some respects that may seem to be in contrast to the Pentecostal roots of Des and Carley Short whose leadership tradition was more apostolic, wanting to emulate the pattern of Ephesians 4:11-16.

However Des would light up when talking about servant leadership, and that was where he and Milton would find common ground. Ultimately they both had a Kingdom of God perspective. They both relished an environment where the Spirit of God had freedom to move.

God drew many other talented teachers and leaders to Faith Bible College who were able to equip students to bring in the harvest. One of these talented people was world-renowned Bible teacher, Gerald Bradley. Gerald had been the New Zealand Field Director and National Training Director of Open Air Campaigners (OAC).

OAC, officially formed in 1922, grew from the vision of a young Sydney lawyer, Edward P. Field, who in 1892 began preaching soap-box style in Sydney outside a large central city bank, and at Coogee beach. In New Zealand OAC were strongly supported by the Open Brethren churches.

Gerald had also served as director of the Willow Park Convention Centre for some years. God was breaking down denominational barriers and at Faith Bible College the wider Church was receiving the benefit of talented preachers and teachers who had previously been locked behind their denominational walls.

Another very gifted Bible teacher who joined the Faith Bible College staff was Welsh immigrant, A.L. (Doc) Greenway. In 1934, he became the first superintendent of the Apostolic Church in New Zealand, having been sent out by the United Kingdom Apostolic Church.

Until that time, the fledgling New Zealand Apostolic Church had been under the superintendence of Australia. Doc Greenway had served in pastoral roles and at various Bible colleges in Japan, Wales, Australia, and New Zealand.

One of the statements he made which is well worth remembering when we slip into the habit of comparing our walk with God with others, is:

> I believe that every believer has a work to do for God that no-one else can do. It is uniquely and specially a vocation given to that saint.

We are to keep our eyes on Jesus and His unique calling for us.

While lecturing at Faith Bible College, Doc also pastored a Presbyterian church in Tauranga. In 1964 he had been granted the unique distinction of being ordained as a minister in the Presbyterian Church without attending Knox College, the official Presbyterian training institution.

Jim Hurn was Dean of Students for 25 years, and his wife Kay served as Registrar. They often travelled to Tung Ling in Singapore and other places to teach the Word.

Hessel van Weiren (a student in 1977) recollects:

> Jim's teaching was biblically based, always practical and always relevant to what we did outside the school in the outstations. He was helpful with our preaching and presenting ourselves.
>
> Jim was interested in people and interested in us. You could go to him with your problems. He and Kay would always be there. Being able to talk to him was a great help to me. It was evident in his family. There was always a tendency in those days for ministry to be first, and then family. But Jim's family was always first.

John and Dorothy Douglas, who had led the Apostolic Church's national training centre Te Nikau in Paraparaumu, served as Academic Dean and Registrar respectively, between 1999 and 2002. John had a gift in teaching theology, often leaving students spellbound with the wonderment of God.

Another former principal of a Bible college who delighted in operating in his teaching gift at Faith was Cecil Mulvagh. Cecil had been the founding principal of the Assemblies of God Christian Life Centre Bible College in Lower Hutt.

These are just a few examples of the gifted teachers and leaders who spoke into the lives of Faith students. The Holy Spirit was doing a unifying work in the Body of Christ as He united various streams of the Evangelical, Pentecostal and Charismatic movements at Faith Bible College.

That unifying work across the Body of Christ was more of a miracle than many of us realised and which we, in this current generation of believers, can take for granted.

Jesus knew it wouldn't 'just happen'. He had to ask the Father for it, as we read in John 17:21:

> ...that they all may be one, as You, Father, are in Me, and I in You; that they also may be one in Us, that the world may believe that You sent Me. (NKJV)

It takes 'the glory', as Jesus continues to say in John 17:22:

> And the glory which You gave Me I have given to them, that they may be one just as We are one. (NKJV)

And it was the worship at Faith Bible College that brought the glory of God into their midst, and still continues to do so today. But God had even more in mind: to thrust out labourers into the end-time harvest.

The Glory

Thoughts to Ponder

1. Consider Doc Greenway's statement: 'I believe that every believer has a work to do for God that no-one else can do. It's uniquely and specially a vocation given to that saint.'
    In what ways are you unique in the Body of Christ?
    What unique giftings do you have? Now consider the loss to the Body of Christ and to the world if you don't walk in those giftings. Does God have anyone else to fill your shoes?

2. Why is worship such an important factor in bringing unity in the Body of Christ?

That's All I Can Do!

In Singapore, during the late 1970s, a group of Brethren leaders had come into the things of the Spirit. Initially they tried to stay connected to their Brethren church in the hope that they could influence them. But this didn't go as well as they had expected.

Des Short began ministering among these leaders and started travelling there three times a year. One of the leaders, Elder Goh, took a shine to Des. He organised a large conference because he wanted to bring together people from many different churches, and invited Des. The conference was run over three nights.

Des asked, 'Who is going to speak on the first night?'

'Dr Yonggi Cho,' Elder Goh replied.

'Yonggi Cho!' Des said, 'I have sat under his ministry. He's an amazing Bible teacher.'

Dr Cho was senior pastor of the largest church in the world in Seoul, South Korea, and had just built a large prayer mountain containing many prayer grottos. Many Christians took time out at the Prayer Mountain to pray and seek God. For many, it became like a pilgrimage.

Des thought, 'Cho has got something to show for what he was able to do for God.'

Des then asked, 'Who is going to speak on the second night?'

The Story of Faith

'Archbishop Benson Idahosa from Nigeria. He's got a powerful healing ministry,' Elder Goh replied. 'I want you to come on the third night because I know you'll bring the Word of God. You see, the people of Singapore are so hungry for God's Word.'

Des had actually initially refused to go because he felt intimidated. However, in the end, Elder Goh persuaded him to go and he went.

Des joined the committee on the stage for pre-conference prayer. Elder Goh invited him to take a peek through the curtains and there he saw a mass of people with Bibles on their knees, eagerly waiting.

Dr Yonggi Cho was staying in a flash hotel and arrived halfway through the worship service. They took him right up to the entrance of the venue in a huge limousine. He was then led onto the platform. Everyone knew who he was. He got up and preached, but he never mentioned a scripture from the Bible.

It didn't worry Des because Cho was talking about what God was able to do through him with the Prayer Mountain and how people were coming there to seek God. It was a good meeting.

But, according to Elder Goh, who wanted to hear the Word of God preached, it wasn't preached. He sat with his committee on the platform after the service and said, 'I am so disappointed: Cho never even quoted a scripture.'

Des said, 'Yes, but what he was doing was so powerful. People were blessed. They were really blessed.'

Elder Goh wasn't convinced.

The next night more people came. Des was also on the platform. When the worship time was nearly over, a flash limousine carrying the evangelist pulled up at the entrance to the venue. Archbishop Benson Idahosa entered the convention centre and walked onto the platform during the last worship song.

He talked about the amazing healing miracles God did through him. And then he prayed for people and that night many people were healed; they were really healed!

Elder Goh was waiting for the Word of God to be preached but the healing evangelist never mentioned one scripture.

Elder Goh turned to Des and said, 'It's over to you tomorrow night. You *must* preach the Word of God.'

Des replied, 'That's all I can do!'

He didn't have a Prayer Mountain to talk about. He didn't have masses of people who had been healed through him. He was just Des Short from New Zealand!

So on the third night, Des preached the Word of God and many people came to the Lord and received salvation. Out of that experience the need for Bible teaching was recognised.

While Des and Elder Goh were praying together one day, their hearts were quickened by the Holy Spirit to start a training school. With the help of Faith Bible College, a curriculum was developed, and in 1978 the Tung Ling Bible School was established in Singapore.

Tung Ling means 'Eastern Mountain' in Mandarin. The founding pioneers believed that God would train many workers in this Eastern Mountain and send them to the mission field, based on Micah 4:2:

Many nations shall come and say,
Come, and let us go up to the mountain of the Lord,
To the house of the God of Jacob;
He will teach us His ways,
And we shall walk in His paths.
For out of Zion the law shall go forth,
And the word of the Lord from Jerusalem. (NKJV)

Tung Ling leaders describe their school as a school of the Spirit, charismatic in nature, inter-denominational, and maintaining a strong emphasis on the Word of God and the present working of the Holy Spirit.

Des returned to Tung Ling three times a year for 40 years. He often spoke on the Song of Songs, a book of the Bible he is passionate about because of its emphasis on intimacy with God.

Jim Hurn, who was a teacher at Faith for 25 years, also often taught at Tung Ling.

In 1993 God gave a burden to Rev Dr Eu Hong Seng to set up the Tung Ling Seminary (TLS) in Malaysia to meet the growing needs of Malaysian churches. With the approval of the TLBC board, Singapore, a Malaysian board was set up to run the Tung Ling Seminary in Malaysia.

One of the graduate students of Tung Ling was Yang Tuck Yoong. After graduating, he founded and became senior pastor of Cornerstone Community Church, Singapore.

When Yoong founded the church, God spoke to him very clearly and said, 'This church must be about global missions. That is the DNA of the church.'

Since inception in 1995 this church has planted more than 150 churches, schools, orphanages, and Bible colleges in 16 different bases around the world.

But there was one college that was really close to their heart. Yoong explains:

> I have always been a student of the Welsh Revival. I think it is one of the greatest revivals since the Book of Acts. I don't think there was a revival that touched an entire nation like this revival. Every strata of society was impacted by this great revival in 1904 and 1905 through Evan Roberts.

It was a great move of the Holy Spirit. I have always been in love with the nation of Wales. God has put something in my heart, a supernatural love.

Also, Britain has invested so much into Singapore: our roads, our infrastructure, our governance, our Parliament. They gave us schools, the law and they gave us the Word of God. The Lord said, 'You have a debt to pay to the British people for what they invested in Singapore.'

In 2012 the Lord led Yoong to redeem and restore the Derwen Fawr Estate in Swansea, Wales. This comprises the famed Bible College of Wales, the school founded and established by Rees Howells in 1924.

The famous evangelist Reinhard Bonnke trained at this Bible school. The school had been closed down, left to decay and was up for sale.

Yoong said:

The opportunity came to buy the Bible College of Wales. I felt it was our debt to pay back to the British people what they have sown into my nation.

I have always loved Wales and what God is doing in this country. Singapore is the land of my birth, but Wales is the land of my adoption.

When he returned to Singapore, Yoong appealed to his church and, through their generous giving, enough was received to purchase the property. The staff and students continue the legacy of prayer and intercession for all nations. Yoong continues:

I think that the depth of intercession that Mr Howells

reached – I don't know anyone that had gone that deep with intercession: his identification with the people that he was interceding for.

When we inaugurated the Bible College in 2016, Dutch Sheets and Lou Engle helped us with the inauguration, and they both concurred with me that this is probably one of the deepest wells ever dug in intercession.

Thoughts to Ponder

1. Why do you think Elder Goh was so insistent on the Word being preached? Why does preaching of the Word rank so highly in ministry?

2. Why do you think God wanted the Derwen Fawr Estate to be redeemed? Couldn't a Bible School centred on prayer and intercession be just as effective no matter where it was located? Why is remembering and honouring a legacy so significant?

Des Short teaching at Tung Ling Bible School in Singapore in the 1970s

This is That

Ask of Me, and I will give You
The nations for Your inheritance,
And the ends of the earth for Your possession.
(Psalm 2:8 NKJV)

In relation to possessing the nations, Des Short, in his typical prophetic flow delivered this impromptu word in 2021:

> When Jesus was on earth a scripture that was quickened to him was Psalm 2:8.
> In that Psalm it also talks about how God sits in the heaven and laughs:
>
> He who sits in the heavens shall laugh;
> The Lord shall hold them in derision.
> (Psalm 2:4 NKJV)
>
> And I pray that one of the things that will happen to you is that you will be filled with laughter. I want the school to be filled with laughter. God sits in the heavens and laughs. Amen! He saw what the enemy was doing, but He laughed.
> Psalm 2 goes on to say:

You are My Son,
Today I have begotten You.
Ask of Me, and I will give You
The nations for Your inheritance,
And the ends of the earth for Your possession.
(Psalm 2:7-8 NKJV)

I know you may have heard that before. But this is God's word for *you* right now. You have been begotten for a different day than the day for which Jesus was begotten.

Jesus came down from heaven 2,000 years ago in the economy of God and, that's why – if you go into the scriptures in Hosea 6:2 – the prophet said that after two days God will revive His people.

We are living on earth right now, and two days (i.e. 2000 years) before this, Jesus was on earth. He brought heaven down to earth. Amen.

And it's coming down to *your* earth here and now. That scripture applies to us. 'Ask of me, and I will give you the (heathen) nations for your inheritance.' Let's claim that.

'And the uttermost parts of your earth.' He wants to possess the outermost parts of *you*. There may be parts of you that are not fully possessed by God. But He's going to come and possess them.

Jesus never came to New Zealand when He was on earth 2,000 years ago, but He is going to possess the outermost parts of the earth. It's going to be fulfilled in His sons and in His daughters. He's going to possess the outermost parts. Aren't you so thankful?

You are in the days of the latter rain. So what are we asked to do? We are asked to pray for rain in the day of the latter rain. And the Lord will make you into bright clouds. If you think of the clouds in the sky, they all contain one thing: water.

God wants to make you and me into bright clouds that are going to be so full of rain, so full of His Spirit and we are going to be able to empty ourselves upon the earth and give out what God has given to you. But you've got to ask for it!

You've got to pray for rain! Are you doing that? You are living in the day of the latter rain. You see, it wasn't the completion of the latter-day outpouring on the early church at Pentecost. Do you know what happened that day?

The disciples were all in one accord. They were all in one place. Then suddenly there came a sound from heaven. With every move of God, there is always a 'suddenly'. There came a sound of an abundance of rain.

And it says, 'This is that which was spoken of by the prophet Joel: that God would pour out His Spirit on all flesh.'

So the preacher at Pentecost had just seen God pouring out His Spirit on about 120 people in the upper room and he said, 'This is that!'

And he's really saying this was the beginning of that which was spoken by the prophet Joel. God is going to come and pour His Spirit upon all flesh. And all flesh will see the glory of the Lord.

The theme of this coming harvest is urgent to Des, so much so that he spoke on this subject at the funeral service for his wife, Carley, after she went to be with Jesus in April 2021.

The Story of Faith

Des could have chosen any message that one would normally associate with a Christian funeral service. But, in his typical prophetic flow, he spoke the message the Lord wanted to speak to His Church in this day.

When he visited Nagaland in 1982, Des saw how a whole nation can turn to God in a day. This had an enormous impact on him.

In the same way that the Lord birthed modern Israel in a day on May 14, 1948, Des is convinced the Lord can cause a nation to wholly turn to Him in a day.

In Zechariah 2:11 we generally think of 'day' as a period of time rather than a literal day. The Hebrew word used for day in this verse is the same word used in Genesis 1, where it is interpreted as a single day as we know it. It can mean both a period of time and a literal day. In fact, some translations say 'on that day' rather than 'in that day', inferring a particular day.

When Des preached on this passage at Carley's celebration service, he reminds us that it is the realm of God's possibility (our impossibility) that this can be an actual 24-hour day:

> I just want to give you a verse of scripture that would be a great blessing to Carley. It is Zechariah 2:10-11. It says:
>
> 'Shout for joy and rejoice, daughter of Zion; for behold I am coming and I will dwell in your midst,' declares the Lord. 'And many nations will join themselves to the Lord on that day and will become My people. Then I will dwell in your midst, and you will know that the Lord of armies has sent Me to you.' (NASB)
>
> Isn't that incredible? Whole nations will be turned to the

Lord in a day and will become my people, the Lord said. Amen! Hallelujah! And then it goes on to say, and I love this last verse (13):

Be silent, all flesh, before the Lord, for He is aroused from His holy habitation! (NKJV)

We've never lived in a day like this day. We are kind of wondering how things are going to finish. I tell you: our God is a God of good beginnings and He is also a God of good endings. Amen.

Let all flesh be silent. For what is the Lord going to do? He is going to rise up from His holy habitation. What is His holy habitation? It is you and I. It's the people of God. And God is rising up. Amen.

We are going to see tremendous things take place. He is preparing a harvest for us way beyond our wildest dreams. We better get ready because the Holy Ghost says it is coming. Amen.

And I know we have heard those words for many, many years. It is coming. It is coming. But I tell you, the great end-time harvest is going to be greater than anything we can ever imagine.

Whole nations will turn to the Lord in a day. God will pour out His Spirit upon all flesh: all Hindu flesh; all Buddhist flesh; all sorts of flesh, amen, in these beautiful, beautiful last days.

What a privilege it is for us to be living at the end of the age when these great things are going to become such a wonderful, wonderful reality to all of God's people.

The Story of Faith

Thoughts to Ponder

1. On the Day of Pentecost Peter had to say, 'This is that,' to relate what was happening with what was prophesied in the book of Joel.

   In the coming revivals, do you think we will still need to say to people, 'This is that,' or will they just know it is God?

2. Discuss the verse from Hosea 6:2 that Des quotes: 'After two days, God will revive His people.'

   How is God fulfilling that scripture in our day? Think about how privileged you are to be living in this day.

3. Des says the Lord is coming to possess the outermost parts of the earth and the outermost parts of you. Ask the Holy Spirit to show you what parts of you are not yet possessed by Him.

   Now would be a good time to ask Him to possess those parts of you that you have been holding back from Him.

4. Des prophesied that a harvest is coming that is way beyond our wildest dreams. He says, 'We'd better get ready.'

   Are you getting ready? What are some practical things you can do to get ready for such a harvest?

He is preparing a harvest for us way beyond our wildest dreams. We better get ready because the Holy Ghost says it is coming.

– Des Short, 2021

Fired Up

In 1991 Emmanuel Amoah planted the Calvary Redemption Church in Ghana's second-largest city, Kumasi, in West Africa. But God had far more in mind for Emmanuel and this would require special preparation. Around 1992 God visited him one night and said, 'I'm going to send you to a place. It's a faraway country you have not heard of before.'

Emmanuel thought, 'Wow!'

Around this time, a friend who was a student at Tung Ling Bible School in Singapore, told him about how Des Short from New Zealand had spoken at the school. In West Africa at the time, there was little knowledge of New Zealand. They had heard a lot more about Australia.

But in 1994 God made a way for Emmanuel to go to New Zealand to attend Faith Bible College. When he left Ghana, his young wife, Augustina, had only two weeks previously given birth to their first child.

But Emmanuel was aware that God was sending him to Faith Bible College to 'fire him up' as he put it, and he and Augustina were prepared to make any sacrifice.

Emmanuel arrived in the middle of the New Zealand winter and, shivering and shaking in the cold, probably wondered how he was going to survive. As he travelled by bus from Auckland

The Story of Faith

to Tauranga, he saw smoke coming out of the roofs of houses (from their chimneys) and thought, 'What is this? The whole place is on fire!'

On getting to the college and going into his room, he got down on his knees to pray. All of a sudden anxiety fell on him. He thought of his wife and baby and said to himself, 'What have I done?' and 'Why did I come here?' He said, 'Lord, I've made a mistake.' He was struggling.

But soon the Lord started to encourage him and open things up for him. One day the Lord spoke to Emmanuel and told him to go and see the principal. The Lord said, 'Tell Des that you want to recruit some people to pray for the college because I want to visit the college.'

So Emmanuel shared his vision with Des, who in turn encouraged him to go ahead. Emmanuel chose students from various nationalities, including a Russian, a New Zealander, an American and an Indian. Every morning at 4.00 am they would meet for prayer. Then, as they expected, God would come down in a powerful way in the weeks that followed.

During their regular devotion and worship times the Holy Spirit would manifest and some students became so drunk in the Spirit they would have to be carried back to their rooms.

For a weekend ministry placement Emmanuel was given two choices, either Whangaparāoa, near Auckland or the small town of Ōpōtiki.

Emmanuel thought: 'Great, I really want to see the big city of Auckland.' However, he felt the Lord telling him to go to Ōpōtiki.

There they loved this black guy from Africa and his ministry so much they invited him back a second time. Although we may think Africa is the place where the demonic realm is more likely to be manifest, Emmanuel could see the demonic strongholds over this little town.

His meetings became so popular they packed out the hall. For two weeks they met every night and there were many healings and people were delivered from demons. Hungry people would queue on the doorstep of the house where he was staying.

When Emmanuel first came to New Zealand, he said to God, 'I'm not coming back to New Zealand.' However he has now returned to New Zealand more than 20 times.

When he returned to Ghana the church in Kumasi grew and other churches were planted. While at Faith, Emmanuel heard God speaking to him about starting a training centre.

So in 1995, he founded Calvary Bible College, affiliated with Faith Bible College, running a similar programme with a Certificate of Christian Ministry and Diploma of Christian Ministry.

Many leaders have been trained for the Kingdom of God from among the more than 500 graduates from Calvary Bible College in Ghana.

Emmanuel is now recognised as a bishop in Ghana and as a prophet internationally. He runs an annual Pastors and Leaders Conference attracting leaders from a network of more than 300 churches and denominations from around the globe, including Africa, Japan, USA, Canada, Israel, UK and Europe.

He has on his heart to extend the movement to Israel by planting a Bible school there. Although this hasn't come to fruition yet due to the political situation, God has enabled him to ordain some ministers among Ghanaian immigrants there.

It was one of those defining moments, a turning point, for Grant and Jenni Brewster when they first encountered Des Short's prophetic ministry in 1986. Des was a guest speaker in their church and prophesied over everyone with incredible accuracy. This sparked their own prophetic journey and a special relationship with Des and Faith Bible College.

In 2002, Grant and Jenni emigrated to the USA to pastor Island Church, a Christian Missionary Alliance church on Bainbridge Island, Washington. You can see the DNA of Des and Carley and Faith Bible College firmly built into this church with statements of intent such as, 'We desire to be a House of His Glory, creating an atmosphere of praise, prayer, and worship to encounter the Presence of God together. In the Presence of Jesus, we are changed.'

Island Church has been a strong supporter of Emmanuel and Calvary Redemption Church in Ghana for 20 years. This church has provided funding and resources to build potable water bores in many villages in Ghana in partnership with an outreach from Calvary Redemption Church. By 2022, 30 bores had been completed in some of the most remote regions of the country.

As an example, five wells were built in the Wala region in the North West of Ghana. In June 2021, Bishop Emmanuel was received at a special ceremony at the palace of the overlord or king, known as Wa Naa, in the city of Wa.

Emmanuel presented the wells as a gift from God and His Son Jesus Christ. This had great impact on the Wala people, and Emmanuel was presented with a robe and the honour of being proclaimed 'Chief of Water', entitling him a place on their tribal council.

Emmanuel credits much of his success to Des and Carley. He says,

Des and Carley have been incredible tools in the hands

of the Lord. They have consistency. They are always on course. They learnt how to sustain themselves for the long haul. They have touched the world. They missed out on some of the normal social privileges just so they could stick to their calling.

They have touched millions. As a result of my connection with Des and Carley, I have seen blind eyes opened, deaf ears hearing and miracles upon miracles. In Ghana I am now considered one of the leading spiritual leaders in my country. Everywhere I go, people know me. It's all because two people decided to obey the voice of the Lord.

Emmanuel's radio programmes reach millions of people, and God has used that medium to bring Muslims to the Lord, and even to open the eyes of the blind. Emmanuel recognises that there is something very powerful in honouring those who have gone before us and who have ministered into our lives.

Emmanuel is an international board delegate for Faith Bible College, wanting to make a contribution to the next generation of students. When he returned to celebrate the 50th anniversary of Faith Bible College in 2019, he exhorted the supporters and staff to look to the next phase of the college and led a prayer pledging commitment:

We are taking ownership of this. We are taking this to the next level so that Your glory will be filled over all the globe.

The Story of Faith

Thoughts to Ponder

1. Have you ever stepped out in obedience to the Lord and then, like Emmanuel, thought, 'What have I done?' or 'Why did I come here?' and even said to the Lord, 'I've made a mistake'? Discuss those experiences and discuss how it worked out in the end.

2. Emmanuel is very quick to credit his success to the input that Des and Carley had in his life.
   What does it unlock in the realm of the Spirit when we honour our leaders, mentors and parents in this way?

3. Before God, ask yourself, 'Do I take ownership of the ministries or church I am involved in? Or am I just there for the ride? Does God want me to up my commitment?'

Bishop Emmanuel Amoah (far right) entering into the joy of giving water to the Wala people in Ghana, West Africa

Faith In Action

Noel and Edith Morris graduated from Faith Bible College in 1972, and for 25 years they worked with World Outreach in Japan, pioneering in media production and distribution, and resourcing the Body of Christ in Japan with teaching ministries.

After 25 years they were probably used to sticky situations. But in 1992 Noel may have wondered how on earth he got into this one, but he didn't really get the opportunity to say no.

Here he was dressed as a Jesuit priest in black flowing robes leading a Japanese disciple, followed by a parade of children in colourful coats, school groups, teams of youngsters showing off their martial arts, musical groups, and a host of other cultural and sporting groups.

Noel had been conscripted to play the part of a Catholic Jesuit priest who had been part of the early history of the Japanese city of Itami. The procession marched down the middle of the road right through the centre of the city.

The Japanese thought Noel was perfect Jesuit priest material but he didn't quite know what a Jesuit priest was supposed to do! All he had was a Protestant cross around his neck. So – making the most of the situation – he held the cross high and proclaimed, 'Jesus is Lord.'

He recalls, 'I blessed the people on one side. I blessed the people on the other side and I cursed the demonic forces that held them in fear and bondage. I found I was engaged in intercession for the city I lived in and its people, as the parade progressed along the road.'

This wasn't to be the last time Noel was conscripted to march the streets. Just two years later, he was marching the streets again. This time he found himself in Eastern Russia.

A new Bible school he'd had a hand in founding, called Faith In Action, was doing what would have been unthinkable just a few years earlier, before Perestroika. They were holding a Jesus March through the streets of Vladivostok.

This was no secret hide-your-light-under-a-bushel gathering. It was 'out there' and exuberant and just as bold as the Jesus Marches in New Zealand in the 1970s. Noel would go on to organise four more Jesus Marches in the following years.

In 1992 while Noel was on a visit to Eastern Russia, the Holy Spirit gave him a burden for teaching hundreds of young Russians who were coming to Jesus. After meeting pastors in Vladivostok who had a similar vision to train and send out Russian workers, plans to start a Bible school were formed.

In 1994 Des Short flew to Vladivostok and agreed to assist with the curriculum and help supply teachers. The school ran between 1994 and 2010 and, for those 16 years, Faith Bible College sent out teachers to Faith In Action.

Des Short, Pastor Alistair Reese from New Zealand, and Noel formed the international board. Noel would organise Bible teachers from New Zealand, Japan and other countries to assist teaching the curriculum. Over that period Alistair Reese would teach in Vladivostok most years.

Noel often went several times a year and, while residing in

Japan, he would go as many as six times. Des Short often travelled there to teach. The mandate was to provide leaders for the church in Far East Russia.

In 2003, just as the semester was beginning, four carloads of FSB (formerly KGB) lawyers and others arrived at the Bible school campus with the intent of closing down the school, and possibly the host church too. The FSB had a large dossier on Faith In Action with copies of letters, faxes and emails. They had monitored phone conversations, interviewed neighbours, and harassed the pastor of the partnering church and his staff for several weeks.

The Bible school was accused of 'conducting educational activity without a licence'. The case was appealed in the Supreme Court in Moscow, but the ruling was upheld to close the college. However Faith In Action was able to continue to operate when it was re-categorised as a training course within a church. The college operated until 2010 when the partnering church stopped supporting the training course.

Over its 16 years of operation, Faith In Action sent out more than 200 graduates who became involved in pastoring churches, church planting, evangelistic teams, prison ministry, alcohol and drug addict rehabilitation and children's ministry.

The following report from one of the past principals of the college provides an insight into the impact of the practical ministry of the students:

> During the hot Russian summer students from Faith In Action Bible School were given practical assignments for evangelism and they found surprising opportunities.
>
> There are so many unchurched villages in Primorye Region that we could not send students to all the ones

we wanted to. But even our small efforts produced amazing results.

A group of students went to a certain village to do street evangelism. This village is a transit settlement near the Russian border with China, where thousands of Chinese traders pour into the Russian towns and villages of Primorye.

Can you imagine this town, with many people of different nationalities? There are always lots of people in the Chinese market but this day there are more than usual.

The bustle of the market is inviting the shoppers to come and spend their money. The vendors cry out, advertising their products: pies, shoes, clothing and electrical goods. Many products made in China are cheap enough for Russians to buy. But the people from the villages are poor and don't have much to spend.

Suddenly, amid the clamour, there are some unusual sounds. Two men near the entrance have attracted a small crowd. One man is playing a guitar and the other is singing, 'Jesus, my heart is overflowing.' The gathering of the curious begins to swell as more come to listen. Then the song comes to an end and the young man begins to preach. The listeners are captivated by his message.

This is a typical day for most of our students during their outreach. The reports show that a total of about 1,500 people hear their street sermons each day.

Of these, 700 are seriously listening, and 150 accept Jesus as Lord and Saviour. These are approximate figures and unfortunately not all remain in the churches. But the pastors in these villages report that their churches are almost doubled as a result of street evangelism.

The village of Barabash-Levada was known as Vladivostok's main supplier of marijuana. The locals nicknamed it 'Little Colombia'. If someone went there to preach, they would be lucky to get out alive. Everybody there was addicted, even children as young as three. Violence and immorality had touched every family, with child abuse common.

The locals were so stoned that they hadn't baked bread for three years, and children didn't know what bread tasted like.

Then a team of our students was assigned to this village. They thought they would be lucky to last there a week, but now they have been there nearly three months. Seventy-five percent of the people have heard the gospel, and about 30 people have accepted Jesus as Lord and Saviour.

Most importantly, there is now a church in Barabash-Levada. Students from Faith In Action Bible School have pioneered churches in many new regions. Not only have they preached the gospel but they have taught and encouraged believers, and helped the elderly and the poor.

About 80 percent of those who graduate are now involved in serving the Lord. Some are pioneering churches, others helping pastors in established churches.

Thoughts to Ponder

1. After working as a missionary in a particular country for 25 years, you'd probably think that was enough.

The Story of Faith

What lessons can we learn from the way the Lord propelled Noel Morris into a very significant second mission endeavour later in life?

2. Can you imagine a place so affected by drugs that they hadn't baked bread for three years and the children didn't know what bread tasted like?

Doesn't this give you a heart for this lost world and the need for Jesus?

Faith In Action staff and students sharing the gospel in the Chinese Market in Vladivostok

Fully Impacted

Nagaland is a small state in Northeast India. It is bordered by Arunchal Pradesh in the North, Assam to the West, Manipur to the South and Myanmar to the East.

In 2011 the population was about two million. Culturally quite distinct, it is like a country within a country and, in 1982 when Des Short first travelled there, its borders were tightly controlled.

The American Baptist Foreign Mission Society was very effective in evangelising Nagaland when they first sent missionaries there in the 1870s. Today 75 percent of the population claim to be Baptist, and it is said to be more Baptist than the Mississippi. Billy Graham preached to a crowd of 100,000 in Nagaland in 1972.

But unwittingly, the spread of Christianity can fuel political nationalism and political control. In the case of Nagaland, there has been a long-running conflict between the Government of India and Naga nationalist groups, who have been fighting for independence since the 1940s.

A number of the Naga nationalist groups have the slogan 'Nagaland for Christ'. Indian government control has been difficult for the Naga people to tolerate, particularly in the shadow of a failed promise first made by Mahatma Gandhi that India would grant Nagaland independence within ten years of Indian independence from British rule, in 1947.

Other factors have added to the conflict. The line the British drew on the map between Nagaland and Burma (now Myanmar) separated many from their homeland, so that today 400,000 Naga people live in Myanmar.

Nagaland did gain a measure of autonomy and, in 1963, it became a separate statehood with a democratically elected government. However for some groups that wasn't enough and they continued to fight for full independence, resulting in periods of direct rule by the Indian Central Government.

It goes hand-in-hand with genuine spiritual awakening that believers will seek to fulfil the Great Commission that Jesus gave us, as recorded in Matthew 28:18-20. Many Naga believers have been faithful in fulfilling that mandate and have been sent out as missionaries to India and beyond.

India, being a Hindu country, has sought to discourage the spread of Christianity into the rest of India. From both a political and religious stance it is easy to see why, in the 1970s and 1980s, the Nagaland borders had become so tightly controlled.

You may think that a land which had been so impacted by the gospel wouldn't need revival. But history shows that the Church has a very short memory of former moves of God and needs constant revival.

Paul Kauffman, the founder of Asian Outreach, was said to be the first white person to preach there in the early 1980s since India had closed its borders, and since a major revival had occurred there in 1976.

In those days Paul would send out a magazine once a year. When Des read of Paul's experience in Nagaland in the magazine, he cried out to God, 'I would love that. I would love that. Would you open a door for me to go in to follow on from what Paul had been involved in doing?'

A few weeks later Des received an invitation to go to Melbourne to speak at a Bible school founded by Hal Oxley. In World War II Hal had been a general in the army, and when he returned to Australia he founded the Bible school.

Des got to know Hal quite well and was often invited to teach there. On one particular visit, immediately after delivering a lecture, a young Naga man who was a student at the school, came up to talk to Des. He didn't tell Des who he was, apart from saying that his nationality was Naga.

Des continued to make return visits to Hal Oxley's Bible school in Melbourne. The young Naga man was very impressed with Des's ministry and wrote to his father about him saying, 'I have just met this man, Des Short, and he ministered so powerfully to the student body. Dad, you are the only one who could arrange an invitation for him to come to Nagaland.'

Des didn't know about the letter the young man had written, and he didn't know that his father was actually the Chief Minister of Nagaland. The first Des knew of this was when, out of the blue, he received a telephone call from the Chief Minister of Nagaland. He said, 'My son has told me all about you, and pleaded with me to open the door for you to come. I am the only one who has the authority to do that.' So Des received his invitation to Nagaland in answer to the prayer he had prayed.

Des flew into Mokochung, the main urban centre in the district of Mokochung in the northern part of Nagaland. It was in Mokochung that a revival had started in 1976.

What Des saw and heard totally floored him. The Lord had sovereignly prepared the people for a move of God. During the

The Story of Faith

summer months Naga people would often eat at tables outside. As they ate, little birds would fly down and sit on the tables and speak to them in one of the 14 languages and 17 dialects of Nagaland, appropriate to the people at the table.

The birds would say, 'Jesus is coming. Jesus is coming soon.'

Many of the Naga people were forest workers as timber was a major export. As workers walked into the forest to cut down timber from the branches of the trees, they would hear in their own dialect, 'Jesus is coming. Jesus is coming soon.'

This wasn't a reference to the second coming of Jesus to earth, but it was preparing the people for a visitation from Jesus. And so the people of Nagaland were expectant and ready for Jesus to show up one day, when 100,000 met together in an arena for a meeting one morning.

A Naga preacher preached on the baptism of Jesus in the Jordan by John the Baptist, where the Holy Spirit descended from heaven like a dove. As he preached thousands and thousands of beautiful white doves flew in and hovered over the people. The amazing thing to the Naga people was that there had never been a dove in Nagaland before!

Des could hardly believe what he was hearing and the Naga pastors and their wives could see the astonished look on his face. They leant forward, looked him in the eye and said, 'Brother Short, it is true. Brother Short, it is true. We were there!'

On the evening of that day, 300,000 turned up at the meeting. This was no easy feat for the Naga people as they had to negotiate very mountainous terrain. It was a calm night with a bright full moon. The ground was lit up with the light of the moon and their description of it reminded Des of Isaiah 30 verse 26:

Moreover the light of the moon will be
as the light of the sun,
And the light of the sun will be sevenfold,
As the light of seven days,
In the day that the Lord binds up
the bruise of His people
And heals the stroke of their wound. (NKJV)

Then Jesus came and appeared in the sky with his arms outstretched towards them. He remained there until the final 'Amen' of the meeting. When they saw Jesus in the sky, the people fell on their faces before Him.

That was the night revival started in Nagaland. Other signs occurred in the revival. Over a six-week period, there was often a supernatural light that appeared in meetings. This light would light buildings during meetings and sometimes would remain all night so that the normal kerosene lamps were not required.

At that time Des was chairman of the mission Asian Outreach New Zealand. When Asian Outreach started in New Zealand the staff had no offices and so Faith Bible College offered their facilities to the mission free of charge. The college looked upon this as a form of tithing what the Lord had blessed them with.

While Des was in Nagaland there was an Asian Outreach conference at the college campus. Des wanted to get back to Tauranga in time for the final address on the last night of the conference. They asked him to speak about Nagaland.

When he got back to the college in the afternoon, he told Carley what he had witnessed. She said, 'Well, Des, did you see any of those things happen while you were there?' She wasn't mocking Des. She just wanted to know why he didn't see it.

Des replied, 'I can't tell you that things happened like that

The Story of Faith

when I was there. But I had so many people coming up to me, bowing and nodding their heads and saying, "It is so true. It is so true. We were there, Brother Short."'

That evening he went to the Asian Outreach meeting. Des said, 'It was one of the most amazing nights. It was a beautifully calm summer evening and the door of the auditorium was open.'

As Des shared the story of Nagaland, suddenly there came a breeze. It was like a breeze from heaven itself. There was a huge tree outside the office building and all of a sudden it split down the centre. A large part of it came into the building, right in front of the pulpit Des was standing behind.

This shook the people because it was as if God was confirming His word with a sign following.

Des said, 'It was really quite dynamic, what happened, and people were stunned by that.' At the same meeting, Doc Greenway's two sons gave their hearts to the Lord. To Des, this too was a sign and a wonder.

Des returned to Nagaland six or seven times. Sometimes he would preach to 10,000 people at a time and once the crowd swelled to 35,000. In Mokochung, Des would stay with a man who represented Nagaland to the Indian Government.

As India is officially a Hindu country, they were very much against the spread of Christianity. In more recent times, church buildings have been burnt down. When Des visited, armed guards with automatic weapons would guard him as he preached. And as he preached people would come and dance in the presence of the Lord.

In relating this Des said, 'I was much younger in those days, you know. Some of the people were very old and they would dance in the presence of the Lord, just dance around. And when

Fully Impacted

I saw all these old people, I couldn't resist climbing off the platform and I danced with them. They thought it was awesome to see me dancing with all these old people.'

On his second trip Des travelled by helicopter between Mokochung and Dimapur, the most populous city of Nagaland. As he flew over Nagaland, he could see a large church building and large prayer house in every village.

When people were born in Nagaland they all went to church and to the prayer house. It was an amazing thing to see. It was as much as anyone had seen of a nation fully impacted by Jesus. Even today nearly 90 percent of the population identify themselves as Christian.

In those days there was no sealed tarmac at Dimapur Airport and Des recalls that on his first visit by aeroplane, they landed on a grass airstrip. As Des walked down the gangplank, he was met by a crowd with many press cameramen taking photos of him.

They took him to a small building to check out his passport and when the immigration processing was complete, his hosts led him out to the street.

There the largest limousine Des had ever seen was waiting for him. In front of the limousine was a motorcade of 20 motorbikes, arranged in ten rows of two. The riders were standing beside their motorbikes and each rider had a banner over his shoulder saying, 'Servants of the Lord'.

At the rear were an additional 20 motorbikes arranged in ten rows of two. These riders were all women. The people of Nagaland had been told that the second white preacher since the State was closed was coming into Nagaland for crusade meetings and that he would be travelling from the airport through the city at a certain time of day.

People lined both sides of the street and waved at Des as he rode in the front of the limousine with the driver. Des couldn't believe it. He waved at the crowds like the Queen of England.

In relating this Des said he just felt like little Des Short from Tauranga. A nobody. But it was a surreal experience and something he will never forget.

At Dimapur he stayed in the home of a very wealthy Naga man. He knew this man was influential because he noticed that people would travel out from the city to see him to seek counsel and direction for their lives.

His wealthy Naga host asked Des if his two sons could come to Tauranga to go through Bible school. Faith Bible College gave the young men each a scholarship to attend. During the Christmas season that year the father of the young men felt his life was under threat and would not venture out of his house.

One day his wife and family members did venture out, and on the way home they were killed by the blast of a bomb planted beside the road. Carley received a phone call from Nagaland and was asked to do her very best to send the two sons home as soon as possible, but not to tell them what had happened in case they became overly fearful.

Of course when they returned home the two young men were greeted with the horrifying news. As Des recounts the story, the sadness of the situation still affects him today and he almost chokes on his words as he struggles to recount the story without being overwhelmed. Des's wealthy friend built a monastery in honour of his wife, and Des had the honour of attending the funeral.

Continuing the link with Nagaland, several Naga students came to New Zealand to study at Faith. One of these was a young Naga woman called Arenla Imchen, who came in 1989.

Fully Impacted

She returned home to help run the Care Counselling Centre, a rehabilitation centre for drug addicts and alcoholics. When Des made a number of ministry trips to Nagaland, he would sometimes visit Arenla's region and re-establish links with her.

The effect of his Nagaland experience is never far from Des's thinking and he spoke of it often in the following years. It opened his eyes, and the eyes of his students, to God's possibilities.

Thoughts to Ponder

1. Des expressed to the Lord a desire in his heart to go to Nagaland.
   Do you have an example of just expressing a desire to the Lord and then watching Him give you that very thing? What did that teach you about the heart of the Father?

2. Some believers would say it was because the Naga people were former animists that the Lord spoke to them through birds and trees. Do you agree?
   Could relegating particular manifestations of the Holy Spirit to only being applicable to people of a certain culture limit our own experience with God?

3. Has God given you an experience, or allowed you to see something that has opened your eyes to His possibilities?

The Days of Elijah

In the early 1980s Des Short joined a team of 100 New Zealanders and Australians in a healing and evangelistic campaign called 'Jesus Heals' in Hyderabad, India.

They united with local leaders and interpreters to form a team of 200 people. Many sick people came to the meetings believing God would heal them.

On one occasion Des was part of a team which became violently sick with 'Delhi belly'. They had been warned not to take ice in their drinks because in those days ice was dragged along the road and became contaminated: perhaps someone had unintentionally contaminated their drinks in this way.

As Des said, 'We were going at both ends.' They certainly didn't feel like participating in the healing meetings that day. But because they were under the authority of the Jesus Heals Campaign, they felt obliged to attend the meeting. That night, the team saw more healings than ever before!

While there Des re-connected with a local church where he had previously preached. With all the new converts from the mission, the need was seen for a new Bible school and Des was appointed to head up a trust board to oversee the planting of the school.

Des and other Faith Bible College staff members continued

to visit this church three times a year for some years. Through the generosity of supporters such as Malaysian, David Yeo, Des was able to offer several in that church scholarships to come to New Zealand and study at Faith.

This sponsorship programme was called the Sons of David Foundation. One of the scholarships offered was to 25-year-old Samuel Rajkumar Patta (today known as Dr Samuel Patta), who was handpicked by Des to come to the college to study in 1982.

To the students and staff, he was known as Rajkumar. Described as a brilliant student, he was earmarked to return to start a Bible school using the Faith programme. After Dr Samuel's two years at Faith, he split his time between America and India for four years, eventually re-settling in India.

Dr Samuel planted a church in Hyderabad called The King's Temple. Starting with a small group of ten members, this has now grown into one of the largest churches in India with more than 50,000 members across multiple campuses in the twin cities of Hyderabad and Secunderabad. The King's Temple has spawned various churches and ministries around the world.

Before this growth happened, while Dr Samuel was splitting his time between India and America, he was doing well in business. However he did not feel he was prospering spiritually in all that God intended for him and he talks about his struggle and the thing that transformed his ministry:

> Our church was struggling. We had a Bible school that I had to take care of. We had about 40 or 50 students, and nobody paid a penny.
>
> The entire burden was on us to feed, educate and provide for them. Besides that, I had a little fledgling church that I had to take care of.

There was hardly any money. I was frustrated. I was discouraged. I was wondering: 'Am I really called into the ministry?' Many times, I wanted to just give up because you know how hard it is to continue, to put up a face when you are putting on an act. You know what I'm talking about. We can speak the right words. But there was no fruit.

We're drying up on the inside. But we don't want anybody to see that we're trying to pretend that everything is fine. We're doing great, but on the inside we're dying several deaths.

Like many other church leaders in the Third World, Dr Samuel was looking to the Church in the Developed World for provision. He thought his success and prospering depended on that. But then God brought him a revelation of FAITH that transformed his church. He continues to explain:

But then, praise be to God, in God's timing and in His purposes, He aligned us in such a way that right now, I'm enjoying a great blessing of God. There was a revelation that came that aligned us with God.

We came to the understanding and revelation that you don't look to man but you look to God for everything. And as we aligned it and we began to move in the Lord, God began to bless the ministry of the church, which grew from 80 people to thousands. Praise be to God.

We now have several locations that we meet in where we have a ministry, and we have gone to different nations; all kinds of stuff is happening.

I know what it is to be dry and dying, and also I know

what it is to come into alignment with God, and begin to prosper. Hallelujah.

Over the years, Faith Bible College staff and students have given much to the Church internationally. Nothing has been asked for in return. As Des's son Stephen says, 'It was not like Faith Bible College was selling a franchise or promoting a brand.'

The college kickstarted Bible training centres and sponsored individuals to come and train in Tauranga and staff members travelled extensively to teach in training centres and churches, expecting nothing in return.

In 2020 the Holy Spirit started to speak to Dr Samuel about honouring Des and Carley, and about sowing back into Faith Bible College. He telephoned Des and said:

> You did so much for us. You not only gave a scholarship to me. In fact a number of our workers went to Faith on scholarships that you have provided. As soon as we are able we are going to come and say thanks to you and Carley and also to see what we can do for Faith Bible College.
>
> We have one of the largest churches in India. We used to be 45,000 for a number of years. But we have gone way past that now. We are going to come down like a flash of lightning. We want to pay back.

God is stirring something to provide for the next chapter in Faith's story. In these end times, as described as the days of Elijah in Malachi 4:6, not only are the hearts of the parents to be turned to the children, but the hearts of the children are to be turned to the parents.

The Days of Elijah

Siliguri is a city in the northeast Indian state of West Bengal, sitting in the foothills of the Himalayas. Ajano, the daughter of a Naga revivalist who had moved there with his family, was a school teacher, and she started a Christian day school in a predominantly Hindu area.

The school grew to more than 600 pupils and had a powerful influence in Siliguri. It has a reputation of providing an excellent education and Hindu families want to send their children to it.

Ajano married Dutch missionary, Erik Vaders, and when the couple came to New Zealand on holiday they fell in love with what was happening at Faith Bible College. Des was invited to preach in Siliguri and, through this contact, a Bible school was built on the same site as the school.

Des went there twice a year for 15 years to teach, sometimes accompanied by Faith Bible College staff. When Faith team members visited, one thing they cherished was going to the school and worshipping with the children.

In 2019 Erik and Ajano's ministry, the Latter Rain Revival Ministry of the Himalayas, presented Des with an award to mark ten years of faithful service in 'Equipping our workers for our Lord's harvest'.

Faith Bible College International was birthed out of the vision to take Faith Bible College directly to the nations. While it was the original intention to bring international students to New Zealand for training – and there are many advantages in doing this – the expense and difficulty can be prohibitive.

Hence Faith Bible College International was conceived to take Faith Bible College directly to the students in their own nation using FBC's one-year certificate programme and two-year diploma programme. These programmes were first

The Story of Faith

introduced at Siliguri, but have since expanded to Hong Kong, Pakistan, Vietnam and Odisha, India.

The Faith Bible College programme ran in Siliguri for about eight years but for some years now, the Latter Rain Revival Ministry of the Himalayas has run its own programme.

The programme has a major emphasis on church planting. Even after they started running their own programme, Des would still be invited there to teach. He would often teach on the Song of Songs, which he is passionate about.

Here is a snippet:

When Paul talks about the nine fruit of the Spirit and the nine gifts of the Spirit, he's referring to the scriptures in the Song of Songs.

He tells us what the pomegranate is a symbol of; it's the symbol of love. The love of God is so powerful, fire can't burn it, waters can't drown it.

Some Faith Bible College affiliated programmes were formulated separate to the Faith Bible College International umbrella. This includes Calvary Bible College in Kumasi Ghana, founded by former student Emmanuel Amoah; Faith In Action Bible School founded by former student Noel Morris; and Faith Bible College South Pacific which was opened in Papua New Guinea (PNG) in 1998.

The PNG college was strongly supported by former Faith Bible College Board Chairman, Pastor Terry Calkin and the Greenlane Christian Centre. Eventually, however, it was determined that it was more effective to sponsor Papua New Guinea students to come and study at Faith Bible College in New Zealand.

Thoughts to Ponder

1. God manifested His healing power through the Jesus Heals team most powerfully when the team felt they were at their weakest. Have you had the experience of God manifesting powerfully when you have felt weak?

2. After graduating from Faith, Dr Samuel Patta (Rajkumar) experienced a measure of success. However, it was a struggle to keep a Bible school running and to build a church.
   He came to the realisation that he was looking to man rather than to God for his resources. When he set his eyes on God as his provider, things changed dramatically.
   Ask the Holy Spirit to show you if there are areas in your life and ministry where you are looking to man rather than God as your source of supply.

3. One of the characteristics of the end-time Church will be the turning of parents to the children and children to the parents.
   Ask the Holy Spirit to show you spiritual children He has placed in your world to mentor and be a spiritual parent to.
   Also, ask the Holy Spirit to show you how you can honour and bless the spiritual parents He has placed in your world.

Atmosphere of Glory

Although she had received prophetic words that led her to Faith Bible College, the non-denominational nature of the college was one of the reasons why Joanne Weir from Northland, and many other students, decided to go there.

When they arrived, students could sense the atmosphere of the glory. As Joanne says:

> The atmosphere was different to normal. It was like you had walked from a valley up to a high terrace. It was elevated. It was calm and peaceful.
>
> You felt like you were growing, without the outside disturbances and distractions of everyday life. It was the result of the prayer covering over the campus and the students. It was free of demonic disturbance and, although some of the students who came were quite troubled, they were set free.
>
> You felt you were growing. We learnt practical things like song-leading, how to take Bible studies, and even how to be careful with money.
>
> For a young woman, it was so good to have Carley there. She was such a great mentor and role model. She lectured

regularly and her lectures on music appreciation were inspirational.

When Americans (now Kiwis) Linda and David Dishroon came to Faith Bible College for the first time in 1979, they probably didn't imagine spending most of their lives in New Zealand. Since 1991, they have co-pastored a thriving church in Tauranga called Changepoint. When they first came to the college, Linda was immediately struck by the beauty of the campus and the beautiful trees. They had been planned and planted by Carley.

Carley was very particular about what was planted and where it was planted. Her love for the environment was all part of her desire to host the presence of God.

Linda remarks, 'There was something about Carley that endeared us to the place. Even in nature, she was hosting the presence of God here on campus.'

Linda continued to explain Carley's love for the Holy Spirit:

> She hosts the Holy Spirit so beautifully. Sometimes in a meeting we felt the need to move on, but she didn't because her value was the presence of the Holy Spirit.
>
> Carley lingered in His presence and held us back to linger a bit longer. She gave us a touch of the Holy Spirit in that lingering time of waiting on Him in His presence. How in touch we all became.
>
> Initially, when David and I came we had no idea of what was to be imparted into us. When I reflect on what was imparted, it wasn't just a song, it was the King of Kings. It wasn't just a measure of the knowledge of the Word of God, it was the Author of the Word of God.
>
> When dealing with an issue, Carley always turned

everyone's eyes on the Lord when she would say, 'Now what does the Lord want us to do?'

Carley taught us how to get into the Spirit and told us that the Lord will give us His perspective. And most of all, it was her daily prayers; she prayed not only for her family each day but she also brought the names of the students before the Lord.

Former graduate, Paul de Jong, founder and leader of LIFE churches, reflects on the atmosphere he experienced while attending Faith in 1979: 'One thing we did learn at Faith Bible College is when you entered the room, Des jumped on the piano or Carley would begin to sing, and everything would shift.'

Another graduate, Pat Buckley, also remembers this aspect: 'Des would come into class early and play the piano, heaven would open and we would all interact together, waiting on the presence of God as we were transported into another realm.'

The college was bathed in prayer by Carley, Des and others. With the high value placed on prayer and worship, it is no wonder Joanne said the atmosphere was different to normal.

Perhaps Carley's address at the 50th anniversary of the college best expresses her respect and love for the presence of God through praise and worship:

> The thoughts God has given me are to do with praise and worship – two things I really love.
>
> In Isaiah 6:1 we see Isaiah saying: 'I see the Lord. He is high and lifted up.' Amen. And what filled the temple? His train.
>
> But then there is the result of that which he saw, and sometimes this happens.

'Woe is me,' Isaiah cried, 'because I am a man of unclean lips.' For the more you have visions of God, the more unclean you seem to feel.

It's funny how that does happen, isn't it? But God's precious love – what does it do? It cleanses us from all sin. Hallelujah.

And it would happen that when our eyes are opened and we see Jesus in all His glory that we will sense our terrible unworthiness, our uncleanliness. But the coals of fire will be applied and Jesus himself will pick us up, and our vision of Him will cause us to spontaneously worship and praise and adore Him, the Lord of Lords and King of Kings.

As I was thinking about this, I discovered that there is the possibility of many visions. So I am going to start by saying we have a vision in this process of His greatness. Hallelujah.

'Oh magnify, the Lord with me,' the Psalm says, 'and we will exalt His name together.'

The word 'magnify' doesn't mean we have got to make God big, like we are drawing a picture to show how big He is. He is already big. Hallelujah.

But the thing is, we begin to see Him big. And that's where we fail sometimes. We don't really see Him as He really is.

And then we have Psalm 69 where David says, 'I will praise the name of the Lord with a song.'

And we have been doing that. 'And I will magnify Him with thanksgiving.' And we are starting to do that. Hallelujah.

And Luke in the New Testament records Mary's words

where she says, 'My soul does magnify God the Lord and my spirit does rejoice.'

So the more we see God, the more our spirit rejoices. So praise and worship seem to rise and fall on our concept of God; whether we see God as small; or whether we see God as big, so big that it takes our breath away.

But most of us, unfortunately, see Him as too small. Praise and worship will rise and fall, depending on our relationship with God. Hallelujah. So we've got to remember who He is; He is our Lord and we worship Him as such.

That was the first aspect of vision that I discovered. And the vision of His holiness is the second aspect. We see Him in all His glory.

The same John who lay on His breast or his bosom, later on in Revelation, when he starts seeing him – what did he do? He fell at His feet as if dead. So John saw Him in all the midst of His glory.

When the prophetess Joanne Moody of Agape Freedom Fighters visited the FBC campus to minister to YWAM Furnace students there, she saw angels protecting the campus. She describes this:

When I first came to Faith Bible College to train YWAM students, I believe it was 2018. I had many visitations from the Lord there and incredibly specific prophetic words, as well as seeing the two huge angels on the property when I arrived.

The Lord spoke to me and told me they were sentry angels. They were large – between 30 and 40 feet tall –

The Story of Faith

and they looked incredibly strong. Their expressions were serious. One stood at the front gate of FBC and the other stood on the back part of the property where the cows are. They were equally matched in size, stature and countenance.

When I asked the Lord what they were doing there, He told me they had come in as soon as Des and Carley found the land nearly 50 years before. When Des declared the land belonged to the Lord for His work and the training of many, these two angels were sent by our Lord.

The Lord told me further they were there to guard the legacy on the land: the legacy of Jesus. I have seen those angels continuing to do their job each time I have returned to train YWAM Furnace students on the Faith Bible College campus.

Thoughts to Ponder

1. What importance should be placed on prayer, praise and worship in an end-times missions training centre?

2. Who is responsible for the spiritual atmosphere at Faith Bible College in the years ahead?

3. Carley taught students to linger in the presence of God. When others were ready to break a meeting she would hold them back to linger a bit longer.
   What about you? Do you linger long enough to have an

encounter with God Himself? Do you sometimes leave your meeting place with God before you have received all He has for you?

A photograph showing where one of the 30- to 40-foot sentry angels stands at the entrance to the college (imagination assisted by the afternoon sun streaming through the trees)

Graduates Impacting the World

The Rose Angel

One day in a church in Bangkok, Mai, a young Thai woman, approached a former Faith Bible College student, Patricia Green. The young woman said: 'You don't remember but you came into the bar where I was a dancer, and you gave me a rose and told me that God loved me. That changed my life and was the beginning of hope for me, and a new life away from having to sell my body to foreign tourists.'

After graduating from Faith Bible College in 1969, Patricia Green returned to Hamilton where she and a friend established Landmark, a refuge for homeless girls.

In 1986 Patricia went back to university to further her studies. While listening to a missionary speak about the huge poverty issues in South East Asia, she was greatly challenged.

At the age of 47, and 18 years after graduating from Faith Bible College, Patricia left New Zealand and moved to Thailand to work in the Bangkok slums, in partnership with World Outreach.

After several years of working and ministering in various slums, she became burdened to help rescue young girls and women who had been sold by their parents or trafficked into prostitution.

In 1988, Patricia founded Rahab Ministries, a mission to rescue young girls and women from the sex industry. As well as reaching them with the gospel, Rahab Ministries trained women and girls and helped provide them with alternative employment so they wouldn't be forced back into prostitution.

By 2006 Patricia had placed Rahab Ministries with capable local leadership to enable her to extend the ministry elsewhere.

Relocating to Berlin, Germany, she founded a similar ministry called Alabaster Jar, a ministry which offers spiritual, emotional and practical help to women working in street prostitution.

Many of these women are victims of human trafficking, from Eastern European countries. Gradually Patricia and her co-workers won the trust of the women and girls they were trying to reach. Their nickname for Patricia – 'Angel' – aptly describes this divine intervention.

Through the ministries Patricia founded, hundreds of girls and women have been rescued from the sex industry, have heard and received the gospel message and are now followers of Jesus Christ. Patricia went to be with the Lord in 2015, but the wonderful ministry she founded continues to set girls and women free.

Ambulance at the Top of the Cliff

Karen Lawson was pretty brave to go to Faith Bible College as a solo mum living off-campus with her three kids.

Pat Buckley, a former drug addict and a student at Faith between 1997 and 2002, thought Karen was even braver to take him on as a husband and father to her children, when they were married in 2002.

Faith was driving them and they had the audacity to believe they could make a difference in the lives of a generation of kids who were heading down the same destructive path Pat had been on for a huge part of his life.

In 2002 they formed the Amped4Life Charitable Trust to fight alcohol and drug abuse and addiction, and to help young people make informed and wise choices.

Pat gives his own description of the impact of Faith Bible College:

> Prior to my time at Faith, I'd been caught up in the world of substance abuse and addiction. I was confronted with my mortality in 1995 when I overdosed, clinically dying three times over the period of a month.
>
> I was confronted with my life: choose God or die. God's got an uncanny way of bringing you to the place of brokenness and I recognised in that moment that, without Him, I could do nothing.

During the first of those overdoses, Pat was at the death rattle stage. The death rattle refers to the audible noise of the terminal respiratory secretions which are a sign that the person is transitioning to the final stage of the dying process.

On the second occasion, Pat was sitting slumped over on a pub toilet seat. Seeing a pair of large bare feet, he looked up to see a huge angel extending through the ceiling, towering over him.

Then he heard a voice saying, 'Because you have prayed, I have placed an angel to stop the spirit of death from taking your life.'

But Pat was still in deep bondage and unable to control the

addiction. He had overdosed to the point of death a third time when he heard the voice of God the Father saying, 'Pat, I love you, son. But unless you surrender to me, you will be dead in three weeks.'

Pat continues his account:

> So I took a risk and, in August 1995, I surrendered my life to Jesus, and I've never been the same. How can you ever be the same?
>
> I spent the next two and a half years in a Christian rehabilitation centre in Whakatane, at a place called Bethel House, where the Holy Spirit and Jesus became the most real persons in my life.
>
> One day a friend asked me, 'Pat, have you thought about going to Faith Bible College?'
>
> I thought, 'Why would I? It's full of geeks and nerds and peculiar people.' But then I thought, 'Why not?' So I agreed to come.

Pat went to Faith Bible College for a trial week, during which time he says he felt 'as sick as a dog'. But he knew in his spirit he had to come back. He continues:

> Holy Spirit spoke to me and said, 'Son, if you want Me to use you, you must allow Me to sharpen you in My Word and transform you by My Spirit.'
>
> So I entered Faith Bible College in July 1997 and realised very quickly this place had something unique and powerful which I knew that I wanted and needed, where faith became real and Jesus became manifest.
>
> Words on a page couldn't change me. Only an encounter

with the living God could revolutionise my life and empower me for ministry. I didn't want or need more stuff, more knowledge, more anything. What I needed was Jesus and the Holy Spirit.

Faith Bible College helped me to become part of a family, a bunch of beautiful people doing life together, having fun and growing and learning side by side; laughing and crying with each other as we faced and went through our own personal journey together ... the endless activities such as playing cricket in D-block hallway; night missions to Burger King, with fellow students all buzzing about what the Lord was doing in our lives and navigating the challenges of living together on a residential campus.

We had 135 students living there, along with about 35 kids on campus. It was wild! You couldn't find a place to find solitude. Except for me – I found it down by the pig pen at the bottom of the farm.

We had Ian Butterworth, the Academic Dean, standing in the shadows, a sole sentry, keeping an eye on his flock; students lay prone over the campus as the presence and the Spirit of God descended and ministered life and sometimes deliverance to those as we waited on Him.

Often Des would come into class early and play the piano; heaven would open and we would all enter in together, waiting on the presence of God as we were transported into another realm; students entering into heartfelt worship; the excitement of the privilege of opening up the Word of God and delving deeper into the tasty morsels that Des and other people gave us as we fed on His Word hungrily.

We had duties and work groups. In fact for four years

one of my jobs was feeding the pigs and emptying the rubbish. So I started to identify with how the Prodigal Son felt when he came to the end of himself.

While I was on my knees scrubbing the pig-pen, I heard the Lord say, 'Nobody else is watching. But I'm watching, Pat, and everything that you do is a test to become more like me.'

Faith Bible College taught me to be vulnerable. You see, when you're vulnerable, you're undone. And when you are undone, you're real. God loves real. He challenged me years ago.

God said, 'You might fool others, but you don't fool me or yourself.' I understand that in order to be real, you have to become vulnerable, and when you're vulnerable that touches not only God, but it touches other people as well.

When I came to Faith I was offered a two-year course in Certificate of Ministry Development and also the Diploma of Christian Ministry. But I ended up doing four and a half years for bad behaviour!

When I went to leave after two years, Des said, 'You're not going anywhere, boy.' I was the longest-serving student they've ever had to this day. I hold the record. But praise God I did it!

Out of my negative life experiences, Faith Bible College gave me the focus and desire to start a ministry birthed out of the very thing which had once ensnared me: drugs and addiction.

Des, Carley and the staff gave me the necessary confidence and belief that something good could come out of something bad.

That ministry, called Amped4Life, was formed in 2002 after my time at Faith, to take a message of hope to many who are caught up in the world of misery and torment, ravaged and broken by these insidious and pernicious drugs which continue to flood into our communities.

To this aim I continue ministering into the lives of thousands of young people across our nation, with the intent to turn others away from this path of destruction and point them towards a better life.

I recognise that in my own life; if I fail to help when I see a need and do nothing, I believe I've missed the mark. The Lord directed me many years ago. He said, 'Simply speak the truth in love, and leave the rest to me.'

To which I replied, 'I can do that. I can't save more, Lord, that's your job. But if I can influence one life today for good, that'll do. I'll take one today. I'll take another one tomorrow.'

All of this amazing work happened because of the impact of Faith Bible College which invested into my life 21 years ago. I'm eternally grateful for the influence the staff and the faculty of Faith have had on me and continue to have, even to this day.

Des and Carley have been very close family and friends and I'm committed to continuing this journey with them, and the mission of Faith Bible College to help carry on the amazing work, which I know has empowered and trained thousands of servant leaders who are now in full-time work and ministry as a result of their time at this amazing place called Faith.

You see life sprung forth out of something that seemed dead and buried. That seed was God's eternal Word and transforming power; that seed that was nurtured and grown at Faith Bible College.

In a real and tangible way, Pat Buckley is, as the saying goes, an ambulance at the top of the cliff. He is also an ambulance at the bottom of the cliff as he is – quite literally – a voluntary ambulance officer and sometimes is there to help youngsters clawing and climbing the walls of the ambulance as they experience the horror of ingesting methamphetamines and other drugs.

The Jesus Revolutionary

In 1985 Brent Liebezeit married Vivienne Clements, who graduated from Faith Bible College in 1983. Brent would describe his church roots in a Church of Christ church in Stoke, Nelson, as being conservative and traditional.

It was a great family church with the historical significance of being the first Church of Christ in Australasia. But Brent wanted more for himself and his church and, in 1987, he took the step of faith that Vivienne had taken a couple of years previously, and enrolled for the year-long course at Faith Bible College.

One of the attractions to Brent and Vivienne was that Faith was non-denominational. They didn't want to learn a denominational mould. Brent wanted to escape out of his conservativism and into the mould that God had for him. But it wasn't easy in those days.

There was no government support for the young couple. As Brent puts it, 'We were on the bones of our bum!' God was teaching them how to live by faith.

Brent admits he was pretty green in the things of the Holy Spirit, but he embraced the opportunity to learn to walk in the things of the Spirit at college.

For their practicum Brent and Vivienne went to Kenya on a three-month assignment. Brent, an electrician by trade, was hoping to install solar power supplies in villages, but the equipment didn't make it to Kenya. God had more in mind. Instead God gave Brent and Vivienne many opportunities to preach and engage in children's ministry. It was as if God was setting a blueprint for their future.

In 1988 Brent and Vivienne returned to the small congregation of 80 people at the Church of Christ in Stoke, Nelson, where Brent took on the job of youth pastor.

In 1994 he became senior pastor and he and Vivienne set their hearts on making the church one of significance.

They knew they needed to take their traditional church into Pentecost. Brent says, 'Faith Bible College gave us the spiritual tools we needed to do that.' He and Vivienne so value their foundation at Faith that – 35 years after graduating – they still pray for the college.

It was far from an easy walk. But Brent and Vivienne learnt to persevere in faith and they developed many practical skills along the way.

Today their church has three campuses: in Nelson City, another in Saxton Road, Stoke, Nelson, and one in Lower Hutt, Wellington, with another campus planned for Christchurch.

The church holds core values learnt at Faith; worship being one of those. They have also formed a strong connection with the Hillsong movement, which is well known for its leadership in worship.

They fulfil their aim of becoming a church of significance in their community with various ministries such as the Shine programme which helps at-risk girls, and 24/7, a school chaplaincy programme.

Their church also runs a performing arts school, a Bible school and a business training school. In 1989 Brent and Vivienne founded the Annesbrook Leadership College (ALC) to raise up Christian leaders and offer them practical ministry training. In 2017 this programme was integrated with the Marlborough Institute of Technology to provide NZQA qualifications.

Perhaps the most miraculous transformation that Brent and Vivienne have been part of over the past 30 years has been that of the Churches of Christ in New Zealand denomination, now called Christian Churches New Zealand.

Brent and Vivienne are currently national leaders of this movement of 30 autonomous churches. Through mutual support and encouragement, many of these historic churches are getting a second wind.

Annesbrook Leadership College plays a central part in the focused training of leaders in this movement. The transformation of the Churches of Christ in New Zealand into Christian Churches New Zealand is unprecedented in the history of historic denominations in New Zealand, many of which have become less and less relevant to the world they are living in.

In contrast, members of Christian Churches New Zealand have become more focused and relevant. They have realised it will take, in their own words, a revolution – a Jesus revolution.

The Cook

We all know it's not about the statistics – Jesus is most interested in 'the one'. But when you look at stats of some church movements, you realise that many 'ones' have been transformed.

So it's impressive to look at the annual report of the Life NZ movement 2020 to see statistics such as four campuses in Auckland and one in Melbourne Australia; 1,894 salvations; 222 baptisms; 103,000 reached by the online church during six weeks of lockdown; 8,000 attending a Christmas Spectacular presentation; 7,000 attending Christmas services; recognition of 1,860 leaders in the movement; $10 million given to community mission efforts; 52,000 meals provided in their soup kitchen; distribution of 32,000 Christmas hamper boxes; 3,125 community volunteers giving 26,000 community volunteer hours donated to over 622 organisations and a very impacting TV media channel called Life TV, which reaches more than 1.2 million viewers.

The Life NZ movement was founded by Paul and Maree de Jong. Paul was a student at Faith in 1979 and also served on staff as a cook, a trade he had learned in his parent's catering business. Paul recognises the foundation of FAITH laid at Faith Bible College, as he recounted in 2019:

> It's such an honour for all of us, I know, to stand with Des and Carley and the team. Fifty years of incredible miracles, of things that have changed, really, the whole elevation of the Name of God globally.
>
> And I believe we will never see, never understand the impact of what happens when people give an unqualified yes. And I know that what we're a part of in Auckland and further afield is because Des and Carley said yes.
>
> No 'kind of', 'maybe' or 'yes' to some and 'no' to other things. Just, 'Yes God. If you're in it, we say yes.'

The Story of Faith

Paul continues his account of his time at Faith Bible College and the recent word of the Holy Spirit that transformed the Life NZ movement:

I was 19, hungry for God and hungry for what God would do. It was an amazing thing coming into Faith Bible College, this environment. I've always been in church, but it was the sense of God's presence (here) that caused an awakening within me that helped me realise: if God calls you, you can.

I was riddled with insecurity, as we are in our humanity, and I was constantly reminded in those times that if God asked you to do it, then you can!

Some of you know the ministry in Auckland and how God has blessed it and is blessing it phenomenally. But I think it was 2015 when I had just a time with the Holy Spirit, I felt like the Holy Spirit tapped me on the shoulder as he has often done, and gave me this picture.

He said, 'When you were young and you were learning to drive in those days, there were people that would teach you how to drive in a specially set up car. And that car setup consisted of a couple of brakes (one on either side), a couple of clutches, and some of the real smart ones even had two steering wheels.'

Well I was reminded, because Maree still thinks she's driving one of those cars. When I get a little bit wild the brake goes down and she thinks she can stop it! But it was like the Holy Spirit again, as He's done many times, was tapping me on the shoulder and He was saying, 'Paul, you've learned to say yes and to be obedient, even when you don't believe that you have what it takes if I asked you. But I'm asking you now to pass the steering wheel back to Me. I want another season where I'm not wanting you to do it. I want you to let Me do it.'

And it's an amazing thing, I think. We live life in times where God has been asking us to take the steering wheel, when we've been waiting for Him to do it.

And then when we can do it, He says, 'Now let me show you what I can do.' And we have seen in the last three years more than we've seen in the 24 years previous. As the Holy Spirit again has said, 'I want to show you something of what's in My heart and what I'm able to do because of the foundation of your obedience.'

In spite of attending Faith Bible College four decades ago and achieving so much through the Life movement he and Maree founded, Paul has found that God is asking him more and more to 'go', to follow Him and to utilise what he has.

At Faith he learnt to be who God made him to be, as he says:

There was somebody in our class who was a prophetic person and, not throwing anyone under the bus, but every session had a prophetic word. And I thought: 'That's it! That's what I need to be! That's a real holy man.'

And so I did the study, as a 19-year-old, on how he lived. He was so spiritual that even if we asked him if we could get a ride to get some supplies from town, he would say, 'I'll have to pray about it.'

And I thought, 'Wow!'

The other thing he would do is, when he walked, he just walked really slowly. And so as a 19-year-old, I thought, 'That's it! That's the key to my future! I've got to slow down a little bit and walk really slowly, and just see what the Holy Spirit was saying.' But I got sick of it after about five steps because it took forever!

There was another guy who had a photographic memory, and he would get up and preach the house down and I thought, 'Oh man, I want that gift.'

Then I noticed that he would go out at 4.00 am in the morning to pray in the fields. And so, I spied him out. I thought, 'That's what he does. He does that every morning.' So I set the alarm for four o'clock and went out in one of the paddocks. I remember falling asleep at like a quarter past four and I thought, 'It's not me.'

I'm not saying don't pray. I'm not saying don't prophesy. I'm just saying, I wonder what purpose God's got for you? And I wonder what will happen if you stay on the front edge of what God's called you to do, and not give up?

Des and Carley were forerunners because they stayed on the edge of what God called them to do and didn't give up.

Paul continues:

Lasting echoes come from forerunners, and Des and Carley have been forerunners for so many years, that the echo will only really be seen in eternity. I discovered that every major move of God has a forerunner.

These were people on their knees, often small in number, but desperate in intent. And when it didn't seem right, they weren't giving up; they were just breaking through into the supernatural.

I think we are in a day and an age where things are changing so quickly that much of the Church doesn't know how to respond. And we're becoming overwhelmed by society rather than realising the answer God has.

None of what's happening is taking God by surprise. But God is looking for men and women that will take this season, with a lean-in spirit. Not, 'Oh well, I used to do it, and I've given up.' No, the reach of God is determined by that spirit of a forerunner that goes, 'We're going to give everything to it.'

Thoughts to Ponder

1. Pat Buckley's service to the Lord over 20 years has been amazingly consistent. Pat will be the first to give all kudos to the Holy Spirit for that.

   It can't be an easy task: waging war against substance abuse and speaking into the lives of thousands of young people about their life choices year in, year out.

   Pat's foundations at Bethel House and Faith Bible College seem to be major factors in him being able to do this.

   Think about how important it is to dig deep foundations in your own life. Do you think, perhaps, that in this day and age, we tend to want to short-circuit our preparation at the expense of not building deep foundations?

2. Paul de Jong asks some soul-searching questions. He says in this season God is looking for people with a 'lean-in' spirit. Are you one of those, or do you have a history of giving up on the things God has called you to, too easily?

   No matter what your past is, ask God to make you a forerunner. Ask Him to make you into someone who is going to give everything to the task he gives you. Ask yourself: 'What will happen if I stay on the front edge of what God's called me to do and not give up?'

3. When Brent and Vivienne Liebezeit went through Faith, they felt they were 'on the bones of their bum.'
    This was a period in their lives when they were learning to live by FAITH. Have you been in that situation? How valuable were the lessons learnt at that time?
    More importantly, are you prepared to launch out in FAITH now so God can build new things into your life?

Never Say Never

Practicums were the practical experience part of a course and they have always been seen as an important part of the courses at Faith. Some were ministry opportunities within New Zealand, others were opportunities in other countries.

In the early days of the college, one of the faith exercises involved the students being sent off to a weekend assignment with only $10 in their pockets. They had to trust the Lord for transport, accommodation and food.

Former student Paul de Jong reminisces on this experience:

> I remember one of the things when we were at Faith called Initiative Training Outreach Scheme (ITOS). Basically, it was a weekend that you had to leave college on Friday with no money, and had to come back by Monday with a good report.
>
> The other part about ITOS, I reckon, was that if you didn't make the weekend ministry team where they would send you to churches, then you were on ITOS.
>
> You had to go out two-by-two and you would just, you know, pray, because you were scared. The other definition I'd give to it is this: Introduction To Overt Stress. It was kind of like,

(Student A): 'What are we going to do?'
(Student B): 'Don't know.'
(Student A): 'Well, don't you pray?'
(Student B): 'Yeah. And don't you pray?'
We would be partnered up with people we didn't know anything about. We would just leave, and we couldn't come back until Monday, sleeping under the stars and doing whatever.

James Muir was a student at Faith between 1991 and 1992. He was deeply impacted by his three-month practicum to Asia in 1992, which took him to Singapore, Malaysia, Indonesia and Brunei.

God gave James a deep love for the people of Asia and, although he is now involved in other ministry areas, he is still involved in Asian church fellowships in New Zealand many years later.

James believes that for a two-week practicum you can hold your breath and bear it, without it really impacting you deeply. But during an exposure to missions of several months, the students are far more likely to work out whether this is the direction for them.

Between 1993 and 2008 James took on the role of Student Outstation Coordinator. This was a very critical position in an end-times missions training college. As well as teaching students about missions, his function was to arrange practicums for students with international and local churches and ministries.

In their placements, students would experience ministry opportunities with the support of mature mission leaders and organisations. An example of a local ministry practicum was the prison ministry. Some students would get up at 5.30 am on a Sunday morning and travel one-and-a-half to two-and-a-half hours to share their faith at two large prisons.

To facilitate the work in the prisons by the students and local churches, James established the Prison Fellowship Bay of Plenty. Both inmates and students found the ministry into prisons to be a great encouragement, and it often led to a deeper ministry to bring inmates into true freedom.

James remarks about some of the benefits of the practicums:

> Students would come back changed. One of the big things was overcoming fear. Fear is a major obstacle. When they went into the prisons, they had to confront hardened criminals who had done all sorts of things. But they always came back with a sense of 'wow'.

As well as the important practicums, James believes it is critical that students also have a firm grounding in teaching on missions. The Kairos Course is one such teaching medium that he and others have used to introduce and educate many on missions. This was developed by former Faith graduate, Max Chismon.

Des Short wondered what he had struck when Max turned up on the doorstep of Faith many years ago, fresh out of the army and still clad in army uniform. When he and Max travelled to the Philippines together in the 1970s, Max decided this was the place he was called to. It was there he developed the Kairos Course, which James credits as transforming the Philippines from a missions-receiving nation into a missions-sending nation.

The Kairos Course is now conducted in 90 countries and has been translated into more than 30 different languages.

The Story of Faith

In 1980 Joanne Weir went on an outreach to Tonga with seven of her classmates. This was her first missions experience and she admits to experiencing culture shock.

The Tongatapu Anglican School principal allowed two of the classes from that school to attend the outreach meetings in the gymnasium. However the teachers were also curious and brought several more classes. It was so full students were sitting everywhere; on desks and every available place on the floor. The gymnasium was packed.

The team presented songs and skits and shared testimonies. They then made an appeal for the children to follow Jesus, and 90 percent responded. The team was so surprised at the response they slowed down and expanded the teaching on becoming a Christian. Then they gave the appeal again and received the same response with 200 students indicating they wanted to make Jesus Lord of their lives.

In 1977 Nick Klinkenberg and a team went on a mission trip to Fiji for their practicum. The culture shock was overwhelming for Nick and, one day he sat on a hill and had a 'woe is me' pity party.

It might have been the scorching hot goat curries. It might have been the experience of being whisked away in the middle of the night to strange little villages and not knowing where you were. Or it might have been the experience of trying to keep up with the irrepressible dynamo, Indian AOG Pastor Nathaniel, which in itself might have been enough to give the most experienced missionary culture shock.

Inwardly Nick vowed to never become a missionary. But you never say 'never' to God! Especially after you have already said, 'Jesus is Lord of my life.' So, after 25 years planting and growing churches in New Zealand, God sent Nick and his wife Karen, also of the class of 1977, as missionaries to Europe for three years, followed by numerous return visits.

The burden for Europe became so overwhelming for Nick that this overrode any mission phobia. Even ten years before he went there, he was printing pamphlets highlighting the plight of Europe with its low rate of born-again believers, to raise the level of prayer for that needy continent.

This was a venture of FAITH he had first seen modelled by Des and Carley at Faith Bible College, and adopted as a major theme of his own walk with God. It wasn't uncommon to find the word *FAITH* written boldly and double-underlined in Nick's diary.

God responded by giving Nick a strategy for Europe. It happened one day while he was deep in prayer. No, it didn't!

One evening while Karen was out of the house, Nick was 'chilling out', sitting up in bed listening to Canadian diva, Celine Dion, blasting out some meteoric notes on his sound system.

There was a pile of church growth books on the floor beside him and he was avidly consuming them, searching for answers. As is so often the case we hear the voice of the Holy Spirit when we are relaxed and 'chilling out'.

All of a sudden Nick had that eureka moment and burst out: 'That's it. It's multiplication!' The outburst could even be heard above Celine Dion's window-rattling ballads by his visitor who just happened to turn up at this significant juncture.

The strategy was to plant churches that had church-planting as part of their core DNA. These new churches would go on to plant other churches and so multiply, rather than add. And so a network of churches was established in Belgium, the Netherlands and France.

Others running with the vision helped plant and run the

Community Planting Training Centre, a church-planting school in the Netherlands. The movement also influenced others in UK, Ireland, Spain, Italy and Poland.

Not content that the strategy was just a model for Europe, Nick felt it could also be applied elsewhere. So in 2020, with other like-minded leaders he helped form a network of churches in New Zealand committed to multiplication. Called the Multiplication Network, this network incorporated churches of any size, including micro-churches.

The micro-church movement has often been seen to be on the fringes by the Body of Christ in New Zealand, even though for many places in the world it is a life-giving necessity. Nick has been able to inject apostolic leadership into this fledging movement and provide connections to the wider body as is essential for healthy growth.

For many students, the short-term mission practicums were a launching-pad to a lifetime of missionary endeavours. Many went on to serve with mission organisations such as YWAM, World Outreach, Asian Outreach and Assemblies of God Missions.

The relationship between Faith Bible College and Asian Outreach was a particularly special one. There was a God-given synergy between the two organisations.

At the invitation of founder Paul Kauffman, Des Short served as chairman of the Asian Outreach New Zealand board for 30 years. James Muir was on the board of Asian Outreach for 20 years after he joined in 1999 and then, upon encouragement from Des Short, James served as New Zealand director between 2005 and 2009.

Bryan Johnson, a student at Faith in 1974, was invited by Des to be New Zealand director, and for the first two years travelled the country at his own expense to impart the vision of

Asian Outreach. Bryan had been inspired when he heard Paul Kauffman speak in a house meeting in 1971. Bryan would often preach on Isaiah 54:1:

'Sing, O barren,
You who have not borne!
Break forth into singing, and cry aloud,
You who have not laboured with child!
For more are the children of the desolate
Than the children of the married woman,' says the Lord.
(NKJV)

He would share the vision that God was going to bless the barren woman (China) and give her many children. He angled this prophetic word in two ways. Firstly, China was a 'barren woman' and would have many children, and it was an opportunity for us to give finances to provide Bibles for these 'children' when they would respond to the gospel in the future.

Secondly, the Church in New Zealand needed to prepare to receive many new children into their fellowships.

Other graduates who served as directors of Asian Outreach New Zealand were Peter Van der Westhuiyzen (class of 1985 to 86) and Kel Steiner (1970).

Graduates who served with Asian Outreach in various parts of the world include: Judith Stanfield (FBC 1984) in Cambodia; Lesley Dawson (FBC 1984) in the Philippines; John and Jean Willocks (FBC 1986) in New Zealand and John and Jocelyn Stephens (FBC 1989) in India.

Many other FBC students couriered Bibles into China as part of their ministry practicum. Once when Des Short was passing through a railway station in China, he heard 'Des Short!'

being called out when a former Faith student saw him in the crowd. Just as he was thinking how uncanny that was, he heard another 'Des Short!' being called out as another former student, unrelated to the first student, identified him in the crowd. Faith graduates impacted that nation and many other nations.

In fulfilment of the Paul Stutzman and David du Plessis prophecies, graduates were indeed thrust to the four corners of the earth inclusive of: Pakistan, India, Cambodia, Vietnam, Hong Kong, Papua New Guinea, Russia, Holland, Singapore, Australia, Japan, South Korea, Philippines, Thailand, New Zealand, Lithuania, Botswana, South Africa, Namibia, Uganda, Jamaica, Norway, Marianna Islands, Germany, Romania, England, China, Cook Islands, Tonga, Israel, Belgium, Columbia, Nepal, Fiji, Kazakhstan and Peru.

There is an end-time harvest.

Thoughts to Ponder

1. Think about and discuss with others the growth you experienced when you stepped out in practical ministry. What lessons did you learn that you couldn't learn any other way?

2. Have you ever said you'll never do something for God and then ended up doing that very thing? Share that with others.

3. Have you experienced God speaking to you very profoundly, when you were just relaxed, 'chilling out'? Why is that?

4. The micro-church movements have sometimes been viewed as a bit of an oddity on the church landscape. Think and discuss how such movements can become more effective through apostolic leadership and connection to the wider Body of Christ.

'To proclaim liberty to the captives, and the opening of the prison to those who are bound' (Isaiah 61:1).
A photograph of Val Bateup, in her early days in Thailand, with Rachel, proclaiming liberty to the captives.

Now It Will Spring Forth

The Lord, through the prophet Isaiah, declared new things before they came to pass:

> Behold the former things have come to pass, now I declare new things; Before they spring forth I proclaim them to you. (Isaiah 42:9 NKJV)

As former student, lecturer and current Faith Bible College Board member, David Dishroon says, 'It was like the Lord was saying, "I personally tell you so that when it springs forth, you will know it's Me!"'

In an address at Faith's 50th anniversary celebration in 2019, David made a prophetic declaration about the future of the college. He was declaring new things before they come to pass, before they spring forth:

> We are proclaiming and declaring new things because the spirit of it is fresh and it's held by the Holy Spirit. And we are custodians of it. There's a shift here today towards a new generation that's coming and we're here to help prepare the way for that.

The Story of Faith

In the next chapter of Isaiah there is a related verse where the Lord is declaring that the new things are happening now:

Behold I will do something new, now it will spring forth; will you not be aware of it? (Isaiah 43:19 NKJV)

Similarly, David prophesied that the new season at Faith Bible College is springing forth now:

We are hearing reports of the Holy Spirit prepping this nation to do it once again. What He did in the Charismatic Movement that made laps around the world, God is indicating He wants to do again.

He wants to use this nation like a womb to impregnate, raise up, mature and again send people to impact the nations of the world. I want to be in on that. Do you? But he says it's going to be new.

To be honest, I can only remember about ten different lectures during the six to seven months of teaching I received when I studied at Faith. But, oh man, can I remember the encounters! Can I remember how I felt – how the Holy Spirit got hold of and gripped our hearts!

And God is saying, 'I want to do something fresh with that. I am wanting to do something new.'

'Now it will spring forth; will you not be aware of it?' God says, 'I want to use you again. I'm not done with you yet. I want to do something fresh and new.'

Meanwhile, in 2019 Paul de Jong also prophesied into the future of Faith:

Now It Will Spring Forth

I felt prophetically for Des and Carley and for Faith Bible College that God is going to take Faith, *not just into a new chapter, but God's going to write a whole new book.*

It's going to be a book that stands on the foundation of what has happened, but the book is going to look different.

The book is going to have things that others can recognise Faith through it, but it's going to have God's purpose all over it and may well not be the way you expect it to be.

I've found that's the way that God moves. As soon as we put our gift around something, God wants to break out of that gift and show us something that He can do and then He wants this thing to step up.

Faith Bible College was a great place of training for that. It's kind of like you were thrown into the deep end.

Thoughts to Ponder

1. To build faith in each other, share your experiences of God announcing something to you and then seeing it come to pass. Then, think of past personal promises he has given to you that haven't been fulfilled yet.

   Is it time to dust those things off and to pray into them for fulfilment?

2. David Dishroon remembered the encounters with the Holy Spirit he had at Faith Bible College far more than what he heard preached.

   Is that your experience? Does that devalue the importance of preaching and teaching?

3. When God does a new thing and it looks completely different to what we expect, how can we guard ourselves from not recognising it and not entering into the new thing ourselves?

God is going to take Faith Bible College not just into a new chapter. But God's going to write a whole new book.

– Paul de Jong, 2019

Part Two

A Whole New Book
Positioning for the Coming Harvest

A Mum's Intuition

Des and Carley Short's son, Steve Short, was enjoying a measure of success in the USA. He had developed some business nous and was doing quite well, thank you very much.

While he appreciated his roots – growing up on campus at Faith Bible College, going to school barefoot with his Māori friends in the little school next door to the college and indulging his passion for rugby – he had no intention of returning to Tauranga.

That was, until Mum (Carley) was on the way home from her daughter Deyon's wedding in New York. She turned up on her 30-something-year-old son's doorstep, and told him he was coming home.

Then she started packing. 'I didn't ask her to,' Steve said. 'She just started packing.' Carley knew something Steve didn't.

Although Carley went home without him, in 1998 Steve did return to Tauranga. He observed the college from a distance and asked his dad the difficult questions.

When Des was 65, Steve asked, 'What's your succession plan, Dad?'

When his father was 70, Steve asked, 'What's your succession plan, Dad?'

Des wanted to protect the charge the Lord had given him

and he wasn't prepared to pass things over until He said so. It wasn't so much what Des wanted, but what God wanted.

When Steve returned to Tauranga God opened doors of business opportunity that you could only describe as miraculous. One of the first opportunities came about through his observation that many of his Māori friends were growing up in poverty.

However he could see that the land they collectively owned was actually very valuable. Valuable, that is, if he could convince a wealthy financier to invest in it. And valuable only if the Māori Land Court, who were dead against such transactions, would agree to it.

Steve travelled to Singapore to try and raise finance. How do you do that? When he heard Steve was Des Short's son, the Singapore-based director of one of New Zealand's major banks granted him an audience. Des's reputation had gone before him.

The banker put Steve in touch with the directors of an international property development company. The deal, though, was teetering on a knife edge because there was no way in the natural realm that the Land Court would grant approval for the development. Even the property development company was sceptical. But – in a surprise ruling – the Land Court agreed to the land sale.

Steve continued to develop property for the next 20 years. He became confident in his niche: he was the golden boy in the Tauranga golden property boom. But in 2018 a major project made a large loss.

The promises and personal assurances he had always been able to keep became impossible to keep. A company he was involved in had to be involuntarily liquidated. Suddenly he was no longer flavour of the day.

But, even in this, God was working. He was moulding Steve in a way we can scarcely understand, shaking him to his core so that he would begin to walk in the unshakable destiny God had called him to.

In 2020, with the drama still unravelling, God placed a resolve in Steve. He could see where the true gold lay. Over the intervening years he could see some things slipping at the Bible college, and it frustrated him.

The frustration level finally got to him and in 2020 he came alongside Des in a very committed way, often ploughing 40 hours of unpaid work into the college each week.

But Steve is not quite Bible school material. He's not what you would describe as Faith 'religiatti'. There again, it was as if he was born for such a time as this and he became a major catalyst for change and preparing Faith for the 'new book'.

In 2021 Steve remarked that Faith Bible College was stuck. It lived in fear of NZQA (the New Zealand Qualification Authority that accredits institutions to allow students to qualify for government assistance while studying). It lived in fear of the government's Health and Safety regulations with which institutions such as Faith Bible College must comply. It lived in fear of spending money.

'People didn't evolve,' says Steve. He continues:

> We didn't plan for future generations. But we have momentum now. We are working out what we can do for this campus for generations to come while my father is still here.
>
> We want to lay out a road map for what happens at Faith. We will not sell an inch of Faith Bible College but we will allow other ministries to come onto the campus here as long as they fit. YWAM has a similar vision to ours, but they are different.

We don't want to lose our way. There will never be another Des Short. He was the visionary. Mum partnered with him in everything. She was a perfectionist, right down to the flowers in the driveway.

They've done 53 years ministering together. Not many have ministered for 53 years. But now we have a group of people who will guide the college forward and protect the legacy. We have got to take it another 53 years. We had become a Bible school – we're not even a mission-sending school at present. So we've got to bring that back to where arrows shoot out over the world as they once did.

The plan here is massive and we need the right people. When I came in here I found an amazing team of people who were paid to work 20 hours a week but who worked 60 hours. They were so passionate about Faith Bible College; they inspired me. And now I am fortunate enough to help Dad steer the ship.

Thoughts to Ponder

1. Look back in your own life and think of those times where God moved you from one place to another. You may not have realised it at the time, but God was working out His perfect plan for your life. Share with others those experiences.

2. Were there times in your life where you were striving for

something and then you realised that the true gold had been right before your eyes all the time?

When you came to that realisation, what difference did it make in your life and to the lives of those around you?

Draw It Near

When the wind changes, we find ourselves in transition as we search for the best way to trim our sails to catch the breeze and travel with the Spirit. The years 2021 to 2023 were very much like that for Faith, and the 'trimming of the sails' included a search for new ways of doing things. Steve Short knew that the way NZQA was working for the college needed to be improved. He was keen to make NZQA a 'servant', using it to hone the college, rather than letting it be a hard task-master.

Steve and Des identified Dr Bev Norsworthy as the one person who could make that happen. Her husband, John, was already lecturing at the college. From time to time, when other work commitments allowed, Bev had volunteered at Faith and they appreciated her abilities.

Bev's leadership in Christian tertiary education meant she had a lot of experience working with NZQA. She understood how to fulfil NZQA standards while remaining true to one's own call and vision.

Fifty years ago Carley's hospitality had played a part in Bev and John getting acquainted. One afternoon during the 1971 Tauranga Convention they were invited along with others to Des and Carley's home for supper.

Not surprisingly, during the busyness that surrounds a conference, they discovered an accumulation of dishes in Carley's kitchen, which they promptly attended to.

During the conversation that ensued over the dish-washing duty, they discovered a commonality of calling. They were married in 1972, and have been involved in Christian education since then.

At the end of 2020 Bev asked God for a verse to guide her in 2021. He drew her attention to Psalm 78:72. Bev entered that verse and some preliminary thoughts about what that might mean in her diary.

Early in 2021 Bev was volunteering at Faith when Des and Steve invited her to work at the college. Her initial response was to decline. However when she went to talk about this with Des he prayed, and in the middle of the prayer he said, 'I believe God has given me a verse for you. It's found in Psalm 78:72.'

So he shepherded them according to
the integrity of his heart,
And guided them by the skillfulness of his hands.
(NKJV)

Bev remembers laughing and thinking: 'How could this be? Of all the verses in the whole Bible, he chooses that one!' But it wasn't unusual for Des to hit the nail on the head with a prophetic word or a verse of scripture.

So Bev accepted the appointment as Associate Principal. As well as ensuring the coursework, policies and documentation meet the requirements of NZQA, she is teaching others how to maintain the accreditation. And most importantly, as these systems are refreshed, she is endeavouring to ensure they align with Faith's vision.

Draw It Near

In June 2021 Des Short resigned as Principal of Faith Bible College, handing over the reins for the next few months to the interim principal, Nick Klinkenberg.

At a special board meeting, Des announced:

The mantle is being passed on. I am releasing my hand from the plough. Let's not waste another minute. Let's get the next stage of Faith Bible College underway together. This is a great day!

During those few months Nick helped to shape the board into a committed and cohesive unit dedicated to seeing the college through to the 'new book'.

In December 2021 Dr Bev Norsworthy accepted the position as the new Principal of Faith Bible College.

When the Lord gave her the promise of Psalm 78:72 to use her to shepherd and guide others with the skilfulness the Lord had given her, she never imagined the full extent of that.

In planning for the future of Faith, Bev draws inspiration from a Māori whakatauākī or proverb:

Whāia te pae tawhiti kia tata
(Explore beyond the distant horizon and draw it near)

She goes on to explain:

It seems to me that God has clearly established the 'new book'. At the moment it is beyond the horizon and our role is to understand, prepare for and implement what it looks like, sounds like, smells like and tastes like in daily life. In other words, to flesh it out or clothe it with visible lives.

Working alongside Bev were a couple who are just as passionate about the college: Dean of Ministry, Frank Sharplin and his wife Aimee, who has undertaken various roles at the college during their tenure there, since 2014.

As well as various teaching roles, Frank was overseeing the practical ministry components of courses and weekend outreach placements. That practical experience was foundational to the development of students, making this role a critical one. Perhaps even of more significance was Frank's gift in worship leading, which helped to perpetuate the atmosphere of worship that is so much part of Faith's core values.

Steve Short identified that Faith Bible College needed to focus again on the original vision imparted prophetically in 1963:

> To raise up an end-time missions training centre, from which literally hundreds upon hundreds of people will be thrust to the four corners of the earth to preach and to demonstrate the reality of the Kingdom of God.

Thoughts to Ponder

1. The Lord guided Bev Norsworthy with both a personal word from the Bible and with a word of prophecy.
   Would you take action based on a prophetic word alone?

2. Why is it so empowering to have a prophetic word that confirms what the Lord is already speaking to you?

3. Are there promises and prophecies that God has given you that you have buried?

4. Think of ways that you can 'draw near' those things that seem to be on the 'distant horizon'.

5. Do you need to undertake a season of training for the end-time harvest? Trust the Lord to direct your paths as you prepare to fulfil His purposes.

*Bev Norsworthy teaching students,
early in 2022*

Free Like a Dove

There is no doubt that the well-respected and very capable Dr Bev Norsworthy was the right person to make NZQA work for the college and make it eligible for funding from the New Zealand Tertiary Education Commission (TEC).

However, by mid-2022, the board realised that, despite the expertise and effort, meeting TEC requirements was actually burdensome for the college, and the system that had to be created was no longer serving to expand the Kingdom of God.

To operate under the TEC framework, large numbers of students were needed to make the operation economically viable, and the board wasn't convinced that the college's one-year and two-year NZQA courses were working well enough to attract new students.

Times had changed.

Prospective students in general were no longer prepared to give up one or two years for a paper qualification. Three-month, power-packed courses, like the college provided in the 1970s, may be a better fit with today's environment.

Meanwhile, Steve Short was hearing the Lord speaking to him: 'Give Me room and I'll move!'

At a board meeting in July 2022, Pat Buckley, never reticent about speaking his mind, gave voice to a bold proposal: FBC

The Story of Faith

needed to break completely with TEC and NZQA and to trust the Lord. The others agreed.

They considered the cost: no more government funding; no more access to student loans; loss of the ability for overseas students to obtain visas for FBC courses. In the natural, these outcomes would be disastrous for an institution like Faith. But in the Spirit, it was a golden opportunity for God to show His hand.

As the decision was made, an overwhelming peace came to each of the board members. Like doves, a pair of fantails hovered outside the meeting room and the Lord spoke a word into David Dishroon's spirit: 'Free like a dove'.

The words that Jesus spoke to His disciples in Matthew 13:52 had often provided counsel to the board to treasure both old and new things:

Therefore every scribe instructed concerning the kingdom of heaven is like a householder who brings out of his treasure things new and old. (NKJV)

These words now seemed more relevant than ever. The Lord wanted Faith to honour the old wineskin and embrace the new wineskin He was preparing.

The board decided to get back to FBC's original mandate:

To raise up an end-time missions training centre, from which literally hundreds upon hundreds of people will be thrust to the four corners of the earth to preach and to demonstrate the reality of the Kingdom of God.

The college needed to be mission-based.

There was also an overwhelming sense that, in order to achieve this aim, Faith needed to connect with the local community and be involved in meeting their needs. It had to put into action the command to 'love thy neighbour'. Students needed to be immersed in that type of atmosphere, and not just limited to a classroom environment. They needed to experience a practical outworking of the gospel. It had to be tangible.

But how do you make such a transformation? It can take years to shed old ways that, although blessed by God in the past, are no longer blessed by Him in the present. God had moved on and the college needed to once again catch His slip-stream.

Not only was change required to alter the dynamic of how Faith operated, but the facilities were in urgent need of upgrade. The board was faced with a project to replace the extensive septic system, and the buildings required renovation.

Another bold and momentous decision was made: the college would have a sabbatical year of transformation and renovation in 2023. That meant loss of very special staff, loss of the YWAM tenancy and loss of income.

As the board made this decision, the fantails returned and again hovered around the meeting room. It was as if the Holy Spirit was hovering over the board members.

But give God room, and He does indeed move.

Within a few months of making these decisions, donations to the college were increasing rather than decreasing. Believers were turning up at the campus and saying, 'Something's going on here. What's going on?' And, more importantly, they were asking, 'Can I help?'

In this time of change, something is indeed going on at Faith! God is setting the stage for His end-time harvest.

Now Is The Time (April 2007)

A song by Deyon Perry (née Short)
Music by Ed Antonio

Had this dream of mine for many years.
Always thought I'd fall and that no-one cared.
I have soared over mountains,
Sailed stormy seas.
Witnessed many miracles,
Now I believe.

Now is the time to see what dreams are made of.
I close my eyes; Destiny reveals its plan.
And if I fall, I know that I'll get up again.
Cause life's too short to let it pass me by.

Can't believe I'm standing in this place.
Feel Your arms of love and Your sweet embrace.
I have soared over mountains,
sailed stormy seas.
Witnessed many miracles,
now you believe in me.

Now is the time to see what dreams are made of.
I close my eyes; Destiny reveals its plan.
And if I fall, I know that I'll get up again.
Cause life's too short to let it pass me by.

The Story of Faith

From here I move,
Don't look behind,
I see horizons,
Now is the time.
Now is the time.

Make of My sons and daughters in New Zealand – ARROWS in My hand!

– Dr Brian Bailey, 1969

About the Author

Garry Rodgers grew up with an aversion to the study of history and literature, instead preferring the sciences, leading to a 40-year career in engineering with 26 years running a small consultancy business.

When Garry was 16 his life had been changed by an encounter with Jesus. This resulted in a growing love for the church, a love for the manifestations of the power of God and a love for missions.

Garry's philosophy had been: why say it in two words when you can say it in one? Writing wasn't even on the horizon until, in 2000, he came across a snapshot taken in Christchurch of Smith Wigglesworth, former All Black No. 10 and revivalist Henry Roberts, and early Pentecostal leader Kelynge England. His fascination sparked, he began researching Christchurch's rich spiritual history, and eventually wrote his first book in 2017, *The Christchurch Revivalists 1850-1930*. The research and writing continued, leading to *Te Waipounamu Awakening* (an account of how the gospel spread among South Island Māori in the 19th century) and *Whatever Wherever* (a biography and collection of the meditations of missionary Haydn Hutton), both released in 2021. *The Story of Faith* is his fourth book.

www.ingramcontent.com/pod-product-compliance
Lightning Source LLC
Chambersburg PA
CBHW062035290426

44109CB00026B/2633